AIM for MILLION$ with Stock Options

The Safe and Scientific Method to Profitable Investing with Long Term Stock Options (LEAPS)

By

Jeffrey Weber

Paperback ISBN: 978-0-9837308-2-8

Copyright and Use Notice

Disaimers

This book is provided with the understanding that I am not giving you legal advice, investment services, or accounting services; just ideas and education. Specific investment questions should be addressed to a stockbroker, legal questions to a lawyer, and accounting questions to a qualified accountant.

I specifically disclaim any liability, loss, or risk, personal or otherwise, which is incurred as a consequence of any of the contents of this book.

Likewise, you get to keep all profits you make from the knowledge in this book; I don't get any of them.

DEDICATION

To my wonderful honey – bunny (alias lovely wife Judy) who has always been there for me and always will be there for me.

Of course I can't ignore my wonderful wife Judy; again she rates more than just being listed in the dedication. My wonderful wife Judy has been there every step of the way for me and helped me through many dark and difficult times. I truly appreciate all the fine things she's done for me, the love she has for me, the love she has for our daughter, granddaughter and now grandson Julian, and the hard work she does. I want to give her the best possible life.

TABLE OF CONTENTS

SPECIAL ACKNOWLEDGEMENT
TO THE CREATOR OF AIM: Robert Lichello

I would like to thank and compliment Mr. Robert Lichello, author of *How to Make $1,000,000 in the Stock Market Automatically.* In 1977, the first edition of that book was published. He devised the investment method I have taken to the next level in the following pages. I'm sure any good bookstore will have a copy or you could order a copy by looking on Amazon or one of the other websites. Mr. L's book planted a seed of inspiration to me like no other investment book I had ever read. I knew it was the right way to invest. It so inspired me that I started investing with the method and started telling other people about it through my own books, newsletter, and website. He has helped lots of people and I hope I am worthy to carry on in his footsteps.

At the time I first read his book, the stock market was going great guns in the middle of a big bull market. The year was 1985. I started charting stocks I liked under the system to see how well the strategy worked on real stocks. From those humble beginnings, my story with AIM began. The story continued under strange conditions about as far away as you can get from the major stock markets – in Seoul, Korea; Maffle, Belgium; and Weilerbach, Germany. It was in those countries where I was stationed by the Army where I continued to learn, invest, and teach what I learned about the AIM method. The beauty of AIM is that it doesn't even require you to be near the market to play. It's so simple and yet so profitable. My hat is off to Mr. Lichello. I hope this book helps spread his fine method to an even wider audience.

I wish to make clear that while the method is Mr. Lichello's, the ideas about using it in this book are my own. If you can think of some way to improve on my ideas, I'd be glad to give you credit in a future edition. Or your praise may go to all my subscribers in my monthly investing newsletter that has readers all over the world. People who have been with me for many of the past 20+ years have seen a lot of fellow subscribers mentioned over time.

I've come full circle starting with a large printed book made 33 years ago that I've been revising constantly to this book you are reading now. I've added information on how to adapt Automatic Investment Management (AIM) for bear markets, how to invest with FAANGs (Facebook, Alphabet, Apple, Netflix, and Google), and the biggest objections or fears to using AIM with options. LEAPS are actually the safest and best AIM investments for investors. But the heart of the book remains the same because it comes from a strong foundation -- capable of handling the job AIM provides in bull markets and in bear times.

Anybody who buys this book can e-mail me and will receive for free the full length and full size 8.5 x 11 350-page PDF version of my original book on AIM investing. Once you buy this book, just e-mail me at jeff@jjjinvesting.biz and tell me you have bought this book. I will be very happy to send you my original book PDF file to you at no charge.

As additional thanks, you will receive a complimentary trial-period subscription to my monthly investing newsletter (a $150 annual value).

FORWARD

Psychology and Emotion in Investing

By R. Jay Hamer, Ph.D., Psychology

Investing money in institutions over which we have little control can be scary. It pokes at our most basic needs for security, safety, and protection. As a result, the markets are often driven more by emotion and emotional reactivity than objective fact.

Is this bad for the AIM investor? Absolutely not. And in fact, as you become familiar with this investment approach, you will realize that over-reactivity and emotionality of other investors is your best friend, and one of the keys to your future success. AIM provides objective, rational direction for your investments amid the chaos of the markets. Most investors see radical drops in stock prices and panic, selling equities out of fear, which causes prices to drop further.

The wonderful AIM approach to investing counsels us otherwise. While it feels good to make profits and increase available cash, the brilliance of AIM teaches us that what others view through the lens of fear, we view through the lens of opportunity. When market prices drop, we have the opportunity to buy at bargain prices, and then wait for the inevitable turn-around. AIM quite literally is the formula for following a contrarian approach to investment, being bold when others are fearful, and being cautious when others are driven by inappropriate greed.

If you have tried investing before and experienced anxiety or even outright fear, AIM is the firm, consistent, steady voice that says, "don't worry, I'll make the decisions for you…relax." This system of investment has been back-tested and validated many times by many people. If you have the discipline to stay grounded and remain patient, you will be rewarded handsomely. The real enemy of investors is not market behavior or financial trends. The enemies are twofold, and their names are Fear and Greed. If you follow the advice of this book and the author, not only will you avoid the enemies, you will take advantage of all the investors that are motivated by them. Reactivity and market volatility will become your friends.

The interesting thing about investing is that, at a deeper level, it teaches you about the fundamental nature of life. Everything and everyone has cycles of expansion and contraction. When you can see these cycles as natural, you can calmly make investment decisions driven by the wisdom of AIM. As you do so, observe human nature as displayed by other investors who are following a herd mentality. They slap negative, scary, or dramatic labels on market trends (such as "bear" market), and their decisions reflect the emotions generated by those labels. As AIM investors, we of course enjoy seeing our profits increase, but we also have the wisdom to see market fluctuations simply as the fuel for the AIM engine, and to see market drops as an opportunity do bargain shopping.

So learn about life by watching the market cycles, and learn how to invest wisely and profitably by carefully studying this book. Better yet, study the book and work with Jeff personally. He's truly an AIM genius, and has incredible patience with those of us (like me) who start investing with little or no experience. Bonus—Jeff has an amazing sense of humor as well! I'm not sure I've ever had an investment conversation with him in which he didn't get me to lighten up and laugh a little—or a lot.

Happy, joyful, and profitable investing to you!

Jay Hamer, Ph.D.

Albany, New York, USA

June 1, 2019

INTRODUCTION

I wrote this book to help all investors – big and small – make money. This simple, easy to learn method will show you an investment method you can use for your entire life.

There are some details I cover in my other books or monthly newsletter such as how to choose a stockbroker for buying and selling under the AIM method. To help you pick the best stocks if you are just starting with AIM I recommend you read my previous book, **Here Are the Customers' Yachts**. In that book I explain the methodology. In my monthly newsletter I give my short list of "best buy" and "good start" stocks that are the best I see for that month. Since you have purchased this book, read through to the end for a special offer to get a "free look" subscription to my monthly investing newsletter.

Please read the entire book and I think you'll agree that I offer a simple, easy to learn, quick method to make the most profits from your hard-earned investment dollars. A note on the examples – some of them use data from a few years ago. These are historical cases that illustrate particular points about investing with AIM. They are timeless lessons that you can still apply today and for as long as the stock market exists.

It also doesn't take very much money to get started as you'll see. On the other hand, if you have a lot of money to invest, AIM is a brilliant strategy to maximize your returns with minimal risk. If you have any questions, I'll be glad to try and answer them. Please email me at jeff@jjjinvesting.biz.

> *Many thanks for your book and newsletter. I enjoyed reading it and found many new ideas I could implement in my own AIM programs. The book was clear to follow, precise and can help the beginner to the system as well as the more seasoned user. It will be a lifelong ally. Thanks, once again.*
>
> Pavlomi T. - India

If you want to have an impressive AIM investment portfolio, this book has been written especially for you. There are many great high-priced AIM stocks with long-term options (LEAPS) like Apple, Alibaba, Berkshire Hathaway, Amazon, and others that are out of reach for average investors. You will see some examples in this book.

One example I will show you is Amazon LEAPS in 2018. It was a flat year for the stock market. You will see Amazon with my improved AIM method grew from $100,000 to $300,000. Then from December 2017 to September 2018 it grew from $300,000 to over $600,000. AND half those profits were in cash!! I hope I have intrigued you to read more!

I want to say good luck with your investing. But the beauty of AIM is that you no longer have to rely on luck! Or chance. You are about to learn a <u>scientific</u> and <u>automatic</u> way to profit from whatever happens in the market, whenever it happens. Enjoy learning!

JJJ

INVESTING SERVICES

LEARN THE MECHANICS OF INVESTING

JJJInvesting.com

CHAPTER 1
Stock Options 101

Businesses issue shares of stock to raise capital for their businesses. Investors buy the shares of stock. Then investors trade the stocks on Stock Exchanges. This trading causes the stock prices to go up and down.

Many stocks also have options. Options give the buyer the right but not the obligation to buy shares of the stock at a set Strike Price. Options are more volatile than stocks and thus their prices will go up and down faster than the corresponding stock price. But when used systematically and safely – as this book will explain for you – they can be just as safe as the stock they represent. Plus they are much cheaper than the stock price so you can control many more shares. The volatility and increased number of LEAPS make them perfect for investors who want to maximize their investing dollars and profits.

When Robert Lichello introduced the AIM method to the world in 1977 with *How to Make $1,000,000 in the Stock Market Automatically,* he used his system with stocks. I have expanded and perfected his strategy with options - specifically, long-term options or **LEAPS (Long-Term Equity Anticipation Securities)**.

LEAPS didn't exist when Lichello first published his book so we can't fault him for not seeing this potential! LEAPS began in 1990. <u>Understanding and harnessing the power of AIM plus LEAPS together will change your financial future forever</u>.

Options can expire in one month or up to three years depending on their expiration date. We will only use long-term options (LEAPS) which expire more than two years in the future when we first buy them. For instance, the January 2021 LEAPS roll out in September, October, and November 2018. You can trade with LEAPS without ever risking that they will expire.

One of the biggest reasons investors stay away from options is that they are afraid they will be caught holding them when they expire. <u>With long term options and my method that is never a risk</u>. In December every year (still more than a year before their expiration) we roll over our LEAPS from one year to the next. Now we have another 2+ years of reliable and automatic trading available to us.

How to roll over LEAPS from one year to the next is covered in my book *Here Are the Customers' Yachts*. Many of my clients prefer just to schedule a time with me in the fall and I walk them through the process with their particular portfolio. This is also a good time to re-assess the portfolio, rebalance it (to obtain a 50% cash ratio for each LEAPS) and sometimes pick other companies when we sell one set of LEAPS. Don't worry if this is too much to understand at this point. I will cover more about all of this in the pages ahead.

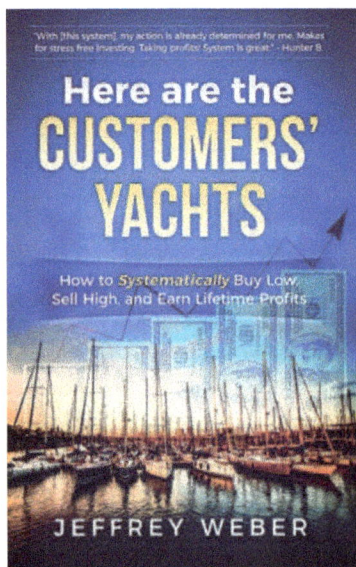

The point is that options are also investing in the companies you want to invest in but you have more leverage and more volatility. For people who want their money to work smarter and harder for them and who have a proven strategy to always buy low and sell high, it is actually foolish NOT to be using options. Long term options or LEAPS are the best of all worlds for stock market investments.

With the AIM method and long-term options, it is fine just to check on your portfolio once a month without worry. But the best practice is to set up your buys and sells ahead of time so that they will happen automatically whenever your target buy or sell prices are reached. That is what the "Automatic" in the AIM method does for you.

You will learn how to do this as just one more reason why AIM with LEAPS is the best guaranteed way to profit from the stock market - year after year for a lifetime.

CHAPTER 2

Why AIM + LEAPS + FAANGS Is The Magic Combination

I am going to show you an investing method that is very safe and makes high profits. My second book, *Here Are the Customers' Yachts,* concentrated on lower-priced options. They are inexpensive so smaller investors can afford them. This book is geared to wealthier investors so I will concentrate on more expensive LEAPS. You will see how well they have worked over both a short period and a long-term horizon.

In order to make the high profits consistently year over year we need to use two things: LEAPS & AIM. When you have more money at your disposal to put to work for you, a FAANG type of portfolio will create big profits on these companies.

Only a fraction of all companies in the stock market have a long-term option or LEAPS. This is a good thing if you want to limit your investing risk. A company with LEAPS has to have a significant level of maturity, capitalization, and history. It would be highly unusual and unlikely for it to go completely out of business! The point is that by using LEAPS with AIM you avoid all the risk associated with penny stocks, startups, and bad stocks. Companies with LEAPS are all highly established, mature, and respected corporations.

As of December 2018, there are just over 900 companies that have LEAPS (911 to be precise). In December 2018 as a Christmas present to my newsletter subscribers I sent them the complete list of all LEAPS that expire in 2021.

If you want to save yourself the time and trouble of compiling this list of over 900 companies with LEAPS, look for my contact information at the end of the book and I will send it to you if you ask.

When you hire me to educate you on how AIM works I will help you select the FAANG and high-priced LEAPS for AIM when you are starting. You will get some ideas of the types of LEAPS I like by looking at the "Big names $ FAANG" model portfolio in my monthly newsletter.

AIM

AIM stands for Automatic Investment Management.   This is an investing method invented by Robert Lichello over 30 years ago.   It's a very simple investing method that tells exactly when to buy, when to sell, and when to do nothing. And it will tell you how many contracts to buy or sell in each case.   This is an investing method that guarantees you **Buy Low and Sell High**.

Three Reasons Why AIM Generates Guaranteed High Profits Over Time

Reason 1: It replaces emotion with logic.

There is no guessing with AIM. There are some judgment calls for the nuances which experience and my services will help you with. But at its heart there isn't any guessing. There is a list of criteria to tell you which investments to make your initial investment into. Then there are rules to determine your price at which to buy or sell, and how many shares or contracts if you are trading in options.

In other books I have written about Mr. Spock versus Dr. "Bones" McCoy. Spock was the rational, scientific character in Star Trek. Bones was the emotional one. Who would you rather be as an investor? I hope your answer is Mr. Spock! That is who you will be with the AIM method.

When you see in my first book that you can make money on a stock that drops 61% below your original purchase price, you know you have a really amazing system. Of course you had to have a fairly tough attitude to hang in there and put that extra $25,000 (or whatever the formula tells you) into the stock. This was done long before I invented a Bear Strategy to handle buys on a stock or LEAPS that goes way down. Now you don't have to add cash -- unless you want to!

Sometimes even when your initial investment is at or near a 52-week low for a company it sinks further. This happened to me with Campbell Resources. But Campbell Resources was still here so eventually the price goes up and that is when all of the leverage you gained with AIM will pay you back many times over with profits.

> *I really enjoy not having to watch my BAC position and worry what it might do. With AIM, my action is already determined for me. Makes for stress free investing.*
>
> **-- Hunter B., a JJJ Investing Services monthly newsletter subscriber**

Reason 2: Some profit comes from interest earned on the cash balance.

A unique feature of AIM is that 50% of your portfolio is held in cash. You might think that this hurts or limits your profits but actually this is key to its success! Besides providing an emergency fund, a hedge against a market correction or crash, and a readily available fund in which you can quickly invest in more stocks or options when prices fall, you can earn interest on this cash. In your brokerage account you can have Real Estate Investment Trusts (REITs) and/or high- yield Closed End Funds (CEFs) with high yields.

Reason 3: Profit comes from the increase in value of your remaining shares of LEAPS.

Looking at one of my examples in a spreadsheet will show you this. By picking companies that are at or near their 52-week low and almost zero risk for going out of business, the initial Long-term options (LEAPS) you purchase will increase over time. As you buy and sell more LEAPS contracts as the price fluctuates, all of the LEAPS you maintain and accumulate over time will increase in value because you are actually holding a portion of these shares as long as you maintain a portfolio in this company.

3 Reasons LEAPS are the "Goldilocks" for stock market investing

AIM is a proven methodology to use with stock market investing. I and many others have been doing it for over 30 years since Robert Lichello wrote about it in his book *How to Make $1,000,000 In the Stock Market Automatically*. But Long-Term Equity Anticipated Securities (LEAPS) provide a uniquely exceptional way to apply the AIM method. They aren't very risky like short term options and they aren't too mild and boring like the stocks or closed-end funds (which are just collections of stocks) that the vast majority of investors use. This puts LEAPs in the "sweet spot" or Goldilocks position for the smartest of stock market investors:

Reason 1: LEAPs are more volatile than the stocks they are associated with.

More frequent swings combined with greater magnitudes of highs and lows means that your opportunities to buy when prices are low and sell when prices are high (only when those prices exceed exact thresholds according to the AIM formula - no guessing or wondering) means that you have more opportunities to profit. Plus because those swings have greater magnitudes than the stocks they are associated with, your profits whenever you buy or sell are much greater than if you were simply executing those trades on the stock. Plus LEAPS cost only about 10% the price of the stock so you can control a lot more stock shares for a lot less money.

Reason 2: LEAPS provide increased leverage for your investing dollars.

Every LEAPS contract you buy or sell controls 100 options. Why buy and sell individual shares of a stock when instead you could leverage your AIM trades by a factor of 100?

Reason 3: LEAPS are long-term options (three years) so there is never any risk that you will be caught holding these options - as long as you follow my method.

I only check LEAPS prices once a month for my model portfolios in my newsletter and they are doing very well. I still advise investors with real portfolios to learn how AIM sets new buy and sell prices after the original buy and any subsequent buys or sells – that will make you higher profits than just checking once a month like I do for the model LEAPS portfolios in the newsletter.

My clients have the benefit of me checking their prices every day just to be 100% sure they aren't missing a trade.

You maximize your profits with no stress or confusion when to buy or sell because your trading decisions are determined for you with a formula. My method tells you how to make these trades with a Limit Buy or Limit Sell so they happen automatically. This means more time for you to spend living your life and focusing on what you care about because you don't care about daily fluctuations or short-term deadlines like all the day traders out there. This is why LEAPS are the most remarkable and smartest investment vehicle to use with AIM.

Most investors don't know about the AIM method. Now you do.

Most investors don't know about or understand LEAPS. Now you do.

Now that you know about both, I hope you appreciate the potential and ability this gives you. But you'll understand and appreciate it more as you read the rest of this book.

Jeffrey Weber is great at explaining a sound investment strategy to help you save for a rainy day and build a legacy for the future.

-- Jacqi H., JJJ Investing Services monthly newsletter subscriber

FAANGs

FAANG is an acronym using the first letter of major high-tech stocks: Facebook, Apple, Amazon, Netflix, and Google (which is now Alphabet). There are other higher priced stocks and LEAPS but using FAANGs will demonstrate the AIM strategy very well.

3 Reasons FAANGs are Exciting and Powerful to use with AIM and LEAPs

Reason 1: FAANG-type tech companies are typically more volatile than the rest of the stock market.

Volatility is what we love to see with AIM! It gives you more opportunities to buy low and sell high. And those peaks and valleys will have a higher magnitude - also what we love to see so we can generate higher profits as we buy low and sell high.

Reason 2: It gives you a way to earn big profits from the tech revolution.

If you want to profit from the tech sector a lot more than being an average investor (or worse, just being a consumer and user of their products) then putting AIM and LEAPS together with the FAANG companies you follow is a guaranteed way for YOU to also capitalize handsomely from the high profits (and the volatility) that these companies experience during our high tech revolution.

Reason 3: Only people with a high net worth can invest in FAANG LEAPS.

If you are looking at FAANG LEAPS, you will probably need at least $500,000 - $750,000 to get my recommended minimum of 12 contracts of your LEAP**S**. Apple (APPL) for instance is about $28.00 per contract in early 2019 as I write this. That means you will need at least $33,600 to buy a large enough number of LEAPS (12 contracts) on the "Near the Money" AAPL Jan 2021 Strike 170 Call to work with.

Then you need an equal amount of cash to manage the risk and trading opportunities in the AIM method. That means you need roughly $33,600 to buy LEAPS and $33,600 Cash or $67,200 to invest in Apple. And that's only one LEAPS – you want to have a diversified portfolio of at least 5 LEAPS, preferably 10. And the more money you have to invest the more LEAPS contracts you can start with. More contracts generate more buys and sells and leads to even higher profits.

Now consider that if you want a well-diversified portfolio of FAANG-type companies, you'll want to have 10X that amount or $500,000 - $750,000 to invest. If you are wealthy you know you need a much larger retirement portfolio for the type of life you want in retirement. AIM is the way to make your wealth work harder and smarter for you.

To escape the higher taxes AIM would cost you because most AIM gains are short-term, a subscriber suggested that people consult a lawyer or CPA and have them set up an LLC company to handle your AIM investing which limits taxes to 20%. Remember my disclaimer, this is not legal or financial advice because I don't know your particular situation.

If you are in a position to have this amount for investing, congratulations on this unique opportunity. That is because even among the few people who are using AIM with LEAPS, even fewer of them are trading at this level. This means you will have unique access and influence on the LEAPS for these companies.

Many of my clients are actually "market movers" on their LEAPS because they are the only ones trading on those particular LEAPS contracts. If you like the idea of being a profitable market mover rather than a market watcher (or worse, a market worrier), now you can be in that position.

Curious what other companies I like for a complete FAANG LEAPS portfolio? The following table is one of the seven model portfolios that my newsletter subscribers see every month (as of 2019). I track and update it every month. As extra thanks for purchasing this book, I have included a complete sample newsletter so you can see all of the model portfolios for yourself.

With this FAANG portfolio of 10 companies, **$1,000,000 starting in January 2016 has grown to $2,698,118 as of March 2019.** That is almost 170% growth in 3 years - and

2018 wasn't a very good year!

Each stock started with $100,000. That means $50,000 worth of LEAPS and $50,000 worth of cash.

In the three years since 2016, using the AIM strategy, Apple went from $100,000 to $277,838. Alphabet (GOOG) went from $100,000 to $205,302. Ahead is the spreadsheet for Apple. Look at the last column in the tables below which shows the total portfolio value (PORT VALUE). You'll learn what the other columns mean and how to use them in the upcoming chapters.

Let's use color highlights for the many benefits of AIM shown in this spreadsheet:

- Apple LEAPS were $35.50 in Dec '17 & $34.83 in Dec '18, a loss of 2% - **But your Portfolio Total went from $267,968 in Dec '17 to $342,689 in Dec '18 -- a gain of 28%!**

- Check February & March (see yellow highlights) to see how AIM makes you profits - **You buy 5 contracts at the low price of $28.65 for $14,325 in Feb '18. The very next month you sell 5 contracts at high price of $42.21 for $21,105 or a gain of 46%. In one month!**

- In Dec '18 we rebalanced LEAPS/Cash ratio back to 50-50. **Our 38 contracts a year now becomes 43 contracts! We are reinvesting our profits to gain more assets and leverage.**

- Even with Apple LEAPS dropping from $40.00 to $24.72 in Jan 19 (creating great buying opportunity) – **in 3 years Apple LEAPS have grown from $100,000 to $277,838 for a gain of 178%!!!**

- Remember in this example I only checked the price once a month. When I help people I check price every day and that makes higher profits with more buys and sells!

APPLE (AAPL) HISTORY WITH AIM AND LEAPS

DATE Col. 1	Remarks Col. 2 AAPL 2020 S 150	LEAPS Price Col. 3	LEAPS VALUE Col .4	SAFE Col. 5	CASH Col. 6	Contracts Bought (Sold) Col. 7	LEAPS Owned Col. 8	PORT-FOLIO CON-TROL Col. 9	BUY (SELL) ADVICE Col. 10	Market Order (SELL) BUY Col. 11	PORT-FOLIO VALUE Col. 14
12/17		35.50	134900	13490	133068	-	3800	134900	-	-	267,968
1/5/18		39.30	149340	149340	133733	-	3800	134900	(14440)	-	283,073
2/9/18		28.65	108870	10887	134401	5	3800	134900	26030	14325	243,271
3/9/18		42.21	181503	18150	120676	(5)	4300	142063	(39440)	(21105)	302,179
4/6/18		33.78	128364	128364	142490	-	3800	142063	13699	Ignore 803	270,854
5/5/18		43.57	165566	16556	143203	(2)	3800	142063	(23503)	(8714)	308,769
6/8/18		49.50	178200	17820	152673	(2)	3600	142063	(25528)	(15900)	330,872
7/6/18		46.93	159562	15956	169415	-	3400	142063	(17499)	Ignore (1543)	328,977
8/10/18		64.30	218620	21862	170262	(9)	3400	142063	(76557)	(57870)	388,882
9/7/18		79.40	198500	19850	229273	(5)	2500	143063	(56437)	(39700)	427,773
10/5/18		80.50	161000	16100	270318	-	2000	142063	(18937)	Ignore (2837)	431,318
11/9/18		64.28	128560	12856	271670	-	2000	142063	13503	Ignore 647	400,230
12/7/18		34.83	69660	6966	273029	-	2000	142063	-	-	342,689
	Roll-over	To	2021	S 150	Call						
12/7/18	2021	40.00	172000	17200	170689	-	4300	172000	-	-	342,689
1/4/19	Strike 150	24.72	106296	10629							

CHAPTER 3
AIM for Wealthy Investors

When you read my newsletter (in 2019) you will see seven model portfolios. There is one portfolio for people who like safety, want to spend the least amount of time trading, and can generate significant profits.

With the FAANGS Portfolio, $1,000,000 starting in January 2016 has grown to $2,447,760 as of January 2019. That is almost 150% growth in 3 years - and 2018 wasn't a very good year!

In the previous chapter I showed you Apple. Next I will show you Alphabet (GOOG). I don't show you all ten because the book will be too long. But read ahead for a sample of my complete newsletter and you will see what is in the entire portfolio.

Each stock started with $100,000 in January 2016: $50,000 worth of LEAPS and $50,000 worth of cash.

In the three years since 2016, using the AIM strategy, **Alphabet (GOOG) went from $100,000 to $205,302.** Look at the last column in the following table that shows the total portfolio value (PORT VALUE). You'll learn what the other columns mean and how to use them in an upcoming Chapter. In this example I am only showing you the final (third) year of 2018.

Once again I will use different colored highlights to emphasize particular benefits, features, and characteristics of AIM.

Date Col. 1	Remarks Col. 2 Alphabet GOOG 2020 S 1000	LEAPS Price Col. 3	LEAPS Value Col .4	CASH Col. 6	Contracts Bought (Sold) Col. 7	LEAPS Owned Col. 8	Portfolio Control Col. 9	Buy (Sell) Advice Col. 10	Market Order (SELL) BUY Col. 11	Portfolio Value Col. 14
12/17		168.04	84000	82507	-	500	84020	-	-	166,527
1/5/18	Ignore Sell	212.00	106000	82920	-	500	84020	(23080)	(12480)	188,920
2/9/18	Ignore Sell	193.00	96500	-	-	500	84020	(12480)	(2830)	179,835
3/9/18		268.00	134450	83752	(1)	500	84020	(50430)	(26850)	218,202
4/6/18		163.50	65400	111195	1	400	84020	18620	16350	176,595
5/5/18		177.00	88500	95319	-	500	92195	3695	-	183,819
6/8/18	Ignore Sell	227.00	113500	95795	-	500	92195	(21305)	(9955)	209,295
7/6/18	Ignore Sell	227.58	113790	96273	-	500	92195	(21595)	(10216)	210,063
8/10/18		326.00	163000	96753	(2)	500	92195	(70805)	(65200)	259,753
9/7/18	Adjust L/C	257.48	77244	162763	-	300	92195	-	-	240,007
9/7/18	Adjust L/C	257.48	128740	111267	-	500	128740	-	-	240,007
10/5/18		245.00	122500	111773	-	500	128740	6240	-	234,273
11/9/18		180.00	90400	112282	2	500	128740	38340	36160	202,682
12/7/18		184.00	128800	76502	-	700	146820	-	-	205,302
	Rollover	To	2021	Strike 1300						
12/7/18		96.00	105600	99702	-	1100	105600	-	-	205,302
1/4/19		99.35	109285	100202	-	1100	105600	(9083)	-	209,497

Notice the benefits of AIM:

- Alphabet was $168.04 in Dec '17 & $184.00 in Dec '18, a gain of 9.5%. - **But your Portfolio Total went from $166,527 in Dec '17 to $205,302 in Dec '18, a gain of 28%!**

- Check March & April to see how AIM makes you profits. **You buy 1 contract at the low price of $16,350 in April 18 – the previous month March you sell 1 contract at high price of $26,800 for trade margin of 64%! In one month!**

- Rolling over Alphabet LEAPS from Strike 1000 with 2020 LEAPS to 2021 Strike 1300 at $96.00 in Jan 19 (creating great buying opportunity) – it enabled us to grow from 7 contracts to 11 contracts which improves our trading leverage and efficiency.

- Remember I only check the price arbitrarily once a month. When I help investors I check price every day and that makes higher profits! You still have profits of 105% in 3 years by checking monthly!

Now let's look at the power of using LEAPS with AIM instead of the stocks. Once you have a method to profit from the ups and downs of the market, which version of Google would you rather be investing in?

Alphabet (GOOG), Stock and LEAPS Prices (Dec 2017 – Dec 2018)

Date	Stock Price	% Change	LEAPS Price	% Change
12/2017	$1,046.40		$168.04	
1/2018	$1,169.94	11.81%	$212.00	26.16%
2/2018	$1,104.73	-5.57%	$193.00	-8.96%
3/2018	$1,031.79	-6.60%	$268.90	39.33%
4/2018	$1,017.33	-1.40%	$163.50	-39.20%
5/2018	$1,084.99	6.65%	$177.00	8.26%
6/2018	$1,115.65	2.83%	$227.00	28.25%
7/2018	$1,217.26	9.11%	$227.58	0.26%
8/2018	$1,218.19	0.08%	$326.00	43.25%
9/2018	$1,193.47	-2.03%	$257.48	-21.02%
10/2018	$1,076.77	-9.78%	$245.00	-4.85%
11/2018	$1,094.43	1.64%	$180.00	-26.53%
12/2018	$1,035.61	-5.37%	$184.00	2.22%
1/2019	$1,116.37	7.80%	New LEAPS	

I think LEAPS should be in everyone's portfolio - especially those with high net worth - because they make much higher profits over the long term than the stock or ETF that they follow. LEAPS are as safe as the stock or ETF that regular investors use when you understand them. You can always sell (roll over) long-term options (LEAPS) when they have one year of time remaining and buy new long-term options that have two years remaining before they expire. People associate options with an expiring investment with a lot of risk but by rolling over the options you extend the expiration indefinitely. You get all of the benefits of volatility with none of the risk!

I hope this helped you decide to use LEAPS with the AIM method. Investing with AIM and LEAPS is how you maximize your profits with minimal risk.

The best way to measure your investing success is not by whether you're beating the market but by whether you've put in place a financial plan and a behavioral discipline that are likely to get you where you want to go.

Benjamin Graham, the Father of Value Investing and mentor to Warren Buffet

Benjamin Graham (1894-1976)

Image courtesy of Equim43 at http://mejorbroker.org/

CHAPTER 4

Why and How to Use 50% CASH With AIM

A person might think that your maximum leverage comes from putting 100% of your investment portfolio into a stock or an option. But this is actually a big mistake.

LEAPS on very conservative stocks such as Amazon, Alibaba, Apple, IBM, can still be extremely volatile. When the LEAPS makes a sudden drop, how will you take advantage of this to buy more contracts?

The answer is the cash that you have in your portfolio!

This cash provides multiple benefits:

1. It provides quickly available funds to instantly pounce on a stock or LEAPS automatically when the price drops.

2. It provides a hedge against a crash should that happen. This reduces your downside risk and exposure.

3. It provides a source of emergency funds if you need to liquidate for some reason.

4. As you sell over time when your LEAPS increase, it provides a way for you to convert your paper profits into REAL PROFITS. Your cash balance grows along with your portfolio value! This also means you are protecting yourself against a market crash as your portfolio increases in value.

A good rule of thumb: if you own 10 contracts you calculate the higher price at which you would sell 3 contracts with AIM and you calculate the lower price where AIM tells you to buy 3 more contracts. Use a 30% drop for the first buy after the initial buy. Then use a 50% lower LEAPS price for the 2nd buy and use only 1/3 of remaining cash. (This in summary is my Bear Strategy.)

If this is too complicated or confusing for you to follow, don't worry. You will see these trades in spreadsheets when we cover the mechanics of AIM investing in upcoming chapters. I also use all of these algorithms when I advise my clients on the best times to buy and sell with their portfolios to use the AIM method.

Hopefully you agree with me that the 50% CASH feature of the AIM strategy is a major part of what makes it brilliant. AIM is a contrarian investing method in more ways than one. Not only do you trade logically instead of emotionally. Not only do you buy low and sell high which is opposite what most people do. You also use cash as your unique advantage to reduce your risk exposure, maximize the speed of your trades which maximizes your profits, and hold onto those profits once you earn them!

CHAPTER 5

FAANG + LEAPS: Proof They Work

Using Automatic Investment Management (AIM) with long-term options (LEAPS) of FAANG stocks is a great strategy for wealthier investors. There are many other expensive stocks that make good AIM candidates. Berkshire Hathaway and IBM come to mind, among others. If you want a more complete list you should talk with me.

As you will see at the end of this chapter, checking the price only once a month from January 2016 to now (January 2019), my FAANG portfolio would have made you 105% profits in the last 3 years.

That's an average of about 35% a year!

Remember you are only spending a little time checking the prices of the LEAPS. In fact there are two ways you can spend zero time: you set up your automatic trades ahead of time. Or you get my help to watch when you should have a limit buy or limit sell. I'll explain how to do this later.

AIM is a lot like backgammon: you can learn to play in an hour or two but spend the rest of your life improving your play. I hope to inspire a passion for AIM investing in you that grows more intense as the years go by. And I want you to fulfill all your dreams.

Legally, I can't guarantee you future profits but I can tell you that the Dow Jones stocks – not LEAPS – portfolio has grown 1,013% in the last 26 years. This includes several very bearish periods like the Dot.com crash in 2000 & the housing market collapse in 2008. I can honestly say there has never been a losing trade with AIM because you only buy when prices are down and only sell when prices are up enough to be profitable. The only qualification - you may have a small loss when you roll over your LEAPS from one year to the next.

Here is a look at the results on my mostly FAANG portfolio from January 2016 – January

2019. This portfolio is tracked and updated in my newsletter every month. Remember 2018 was a year where the stock market was about flat but it led to many good buys:

New 2019 Portfolio Has Chinese, Some Big Names (FAANGS)
JANUARY 2016 - JANUARY 2019

LEAPS NAME	OPTION PRICE	STARTING PORTFOLIO VALUE	CURRENT PORTFOLIO VALUE	% GAIN (LOSS)
CHINA 25 JAN 21 STRIKE 30	10.70	100,000	171,586	72%
NIKE JAN 21 STRIKE 50	28.40	100,000	179,748	80%
AMAZON JAN 21 STRIKE 1800	243.65	100,000	533,673	434%
ALPHABET JAN 21 STRIKE 1300	99.35	100,000	209,407	109%
AMD JAN 21 STRIKE 20	6.52	100,000	42,187	(58%)
TESLA (PUT) JAN 21 STRIKE 210	31.90	100,000	68,971	(31%)
FACEBOOK JAN 21 STRIKE 150	24.25	100,000	117,730	18%
PAYPAL JAN 21 STRIKE 75	23.00	100,000	446,240	346%
APPLE JAN 21 STRIKE 150	40.00	100,000	277,838	178%
ALIBABA JAN 21 STRIKE 150	25.75	100,000	254,172	154%
TOTALS		**$1,000,000**	**$2,047,460**	**105%**

The two big winners were Amazon up 434% and PayPal up 346%. Both embrace new technology – Amazon led the way to shop online and PayPal led the way to send and receive money online.

The two big losers (in fact only losers) are AMD down 58% and Tesla (Put) down 31%. The AMD history is misleading because I originally used a gold stock that lost money so I shifted the remaining Portfolio Value into AMD. Tesla is down in recent months - now way down below $200 a share. A lot of people are skeptical that TESLA can be a viable company over the long term. I agree there is fundamental risk there; such is the nature of investing in that company. But the Put LEAPS are up and getting close to profitable.

Look at the numbers across the portfolio for the last three years and you will see that the results speak for themselves - AIM with FAANG-type LEAPS works to create big profits.

CHAPTER 6

The Mechanics of AIM Trades with LEAPS

Here is how to buy, sell, or do nothing under the AIM (Automatic Investment Management) method. This is an important -- probably the most important -- chapter of the book. You must thoroughly understand and follow this to get the benefits from the AIM method.

I'm going to go through it slowly and I want you not only to read and understand it, but also practice it with some LEAPS of your own until it becomes second nature. And it will! At first it might seem complicated, but it's really incredibly simple.

Once you learn it, you will be doing exactly the same process every month but the particular numbers for buys and sells will be different. Some months the AIM method will tell you to buy. It will tell you how much to buy or how many dollars' worth of option contracts to buy. Some months the AIM strategy will tell you how many dollars' worth of option contracts to sell. Or AIM may want you to do nothing because the price of the LEAPS hasn't gone down or up enough to justify a buy or sell.

Here's how to do it.

GET A BROKERAGE ACCOUNT WITH LOW LEVEL OPTIONS TRADING AUTHORIZATION

The first thing you need to do is open a stock broker account. When you open it you need to tell your broker you want to be able to buy and sell (trade) options. You only need low level option approval (also called Level 1 with some brokerage firms) which is routinely granted after you read the booklet warning you of the dangers of trading options. Level 1 means you can buy options (LEAPS) up to the amount of cash available in your account - in other words you can't over extend your position. On TD Ameritrade this appears on the Positions page. If you have questions or want help with these requests contact me after reading this book. (My contact information is at the end.)

My personal preference for a brokerage account is TD Ameritrade. They have excellent customer service when I call them, reasonable fees, and their website is easy enough for me to navigate for all my AIM investing needs. Considering how technology-challenged I am with computers that is saying something. They aren't paying me to recommend them, but considering how many clients I have brought to them over the years they probably should. The screenshots you see in the book will be from the TD Ameritrade website.

HOW TO FIND THE LEAPS FOR A STOCK

While you are waiting for your option trading ability to get approved you can start looking for the LEAPS on companies you may want to invest in. To find LEAPS I like looking at Seeking Alpha articles (seekingalpha.com). You can receive future email articles on any stock for free by asking to receive email updates.

At the end of 2018, my subscribers got a list of all LEAPS available in the world with January 2021 expiration. There were 911 of them. If you would like that convenient list you can ask me for it by contacting me. I will also invite you to join my newsletter for a free limited-term subscription so that when December comes around you will get an updated list of all LEAPS that exist.

In these screenshots I'm going to use TD Ameritrade because that is where I set up the AIM trades for myself. When the summary page for a company comes up, click on the link for **Options** or **Option chain**. The options with the shortest expiration date will appear. We don't want these options! Click the **View full chain** link to see all the available options. Then Click on the **Expiration** button and you will see a drop down menu of different dates. The options (LEAPS) we want are near or at the bottom.

Once you are looking at the list of options for a company, click on Jan 2021 date (for example) and the LEAPS that expire in January 2021 will appear. These LEAPS will be used until roughly December 2019 and then we will sell them and roll over the 2021 LEAPS into Jan 2022 LEAPS because we don't want to own LEAPS with only one year before they expire.

As a rule <u>you want the January date farthest in the future possible</u>. Notice in the screenshot above the expiration date is March 29, 2019. You don't want that because it is much too soon (actually impossible by the time this book is published). When you view the full chain you will fix that (and I will show you how shortly).

Next I usually recommend <u>sticking with Calls</u>. You buy Calls because you are bullish on the stock & economy and think the stock will go up. (When you use my strategy to always make your first buy at or near the 52-week low you are much more likely to be right!)

Now we have to choose a Strike Price. The Strike Price is the amount you could buy 100 options at any time up until the LEAPS expire. We are only trading the LEAPS contracts – we will never take delivery of the stock – that is for a different type of investor. I recommend <u>picking a Strike Price at or near what the stock is selling at.</u> For example, if Amazon is selling at $1,600 a share, then pick a Strike Price of 1700 or 1800.

Side note - picking a Strike Price below the stock price is called **"In the Money."** Picking a Strike Price above the stock price is called **"Out of the Money."** Explaining the rationale and pros / cons for these strategies is beyond the scope of this book but is summarized in my first book. Contact me to get your free copy of that as a PDF or hire me as your investing advisor and I will be glad to explain this to you and consider them for your particular investment choices and objectives.

WHEN TO MAKE YOUR FIRST BUY

Once you have your list of LEAPS you want to invest in, I'm sure you want to get started. But the secret of the AIM strategy is to BUY LOW and SELL HIGH. That means you want to <u>make your first buy when your stock or LEAPS is at or near its 52-week low.</u>

Don't worry if you only have the money to buy one or two LEAPS. The most important advice I can give you is start now learning AIM. You will have more money in the future from AIM and job promotions so you can add more LEAPS in the future and have a more diversified portfolio. The important thing is to start learning AIM and "having skin in the game" by owning LEAPS. AIM is always the same method so it is just as easy to learn with one LEAPS as with 10 LEAPS!

If you want help finding more LEAPS that are good to buy right now you can ask me. My monthly newsletter has a list that I update every single month. If you aren't subscribed to my newsletter yet contact me through my website or my contact information at the end of the book and I will send you my next issue for free. (I might still have the offer of a "free look" subscription period.)

HOW MANY LEAPS TO BUY ON YOUR FIRST TRADE

You want to be able to <u>buy at least 10 contracts</u> so you will be able to trade contracts and make money. But <u>15-20 contracts is even better</u> if you can afford it. The amount of money you will be starting with will determine what LEAPS price you should buy.

Here is something very important and unique about the AIM method: <u>you must keep an equivalent amount of cash in your portfolio for every stock (LEAPS) you invest in</u>!

One other very important calculation: <u>every LEAPS contract actually has 100 options</u>!

For example – **if you have $1,000,000 to invest in a company then you want to buy $500,000 worth of LEAPS. So you can buy a LEAPS worth up to $500.** The contract will be $500x100 or $50,000. Then 10 of those contracts will be $500,000.

Option prices get lower the more Out of the Money the Call option is. So if the stock price is $1,600, the Strike 1500 option contract might be $50,000. The Strike 1600 option contract might be $40,000, and the Strike 1700 option contract might be $30,000. Remember, one LEAPS contract contains 100 options.

This gets a little complicated for beginners so I invite you to hire me for 6 months of management services to help you learn to manage your portfolio after you get started and show you how to trade using my AIM method for 6 months. Then you will thoroughly understand this investing method and easily be able to do it yourself. Of course I am happy to continue helping you with your portfolio. Again I am trying to give you enough information so you know when you need to ask me a question. Everybody has a different level of investing knowledge. I don't want investing novices to be scared – this is easy to learn with my help and will make you very high profits on very safe investments.

SETTING UP YOUR AIM SPREADSHEET

I will walk you through an example from 2017-2018. The way AIM works is timeless so this is still a good example. As long as prices are moving up or down or holding steady the

AIM method tells you when to buy or sell, how much to buy and sell, or when to do nothing. This stays the same year after year. When you receive your free look at my monthly newsletter you will get the very latest numbers in several portfolios and you will see that AIM is still earning great profits after all these years. (I started my newsletter in 1993.)

Imagine if you had started using this method 15+ years ago when LEAPS were invented. Don't have the same regret 20 years from now.

There still may be some old-fashioned investors who don't like computers so this will appeal to them. I have created a Word and Excel version of the LEAPS spreadsheet you can print out and you can easily do all of these calculations on paper if you prefer. Doing it yourself is the best way to learn AIM.

I recommend you print out the blank spreadsheet, copy the first row from the finished spreadsheet, and then copy the date and LEAPS price columns. Then do the calculations yourself. When you get the same numbers as the example here you understand how to do AIM.

Now a quick explanation of what every column means before we look at almost one year of transactions and you see AIM in action.

Column 1 DATE - The date becomes the month and year (for example 6/16.) You check your stock or LEAPS at least monthly. It is much better to have automatic notifications set up to alert you to changes. When I work as your advisor I check your prices daily. In this example I am just going to be checking the LEAPS monthly. And you will see just checking monthly can still make you quite a nice profit. So 6/16 would be followed by 7/16, followed by 8/16 - I think you get the picture.

Column 2 REMARKS - Here you will list things such as readjust stock/cash ratio or stock splits. I change these if I am using a Bear strategy in a bear market. That's a topic for later.

Column 3 – LEAPS PRICE - This is the closing price of one long-term option (LEAPS) as reported in the newspaper or the website or your broker for the day you're checking. You can easily find daily prices online. **IMPORTANT: YOU WANT TO LOOK UP THE <u>THEORETICAL PRICE</u> BECAUSE IT'S THE MOST ACCURATE PRICE**

AT ANY GIVEN MOMENT!

Column 4 – LEAPS VALUE - This is the LEAPS PRICE from column 3 multiplied by the number of LEAPS OWNED which is found in column 8.

Column 5 SAFE – SAFE is 10% of the LEAPS value found in column 2. Thus, if your LEAPS VALUE is $50,000, your SAFE amount would be $5,000. You'll see how SAFE keeps you from buying and selling too soon when we go through the actual LEAPS example.

Column 6 – CASH - Originally Robert Lichello said to use a ratio of 50% CASH and 50% shares when you start an AIM investment. So for example, if you started with $200,000, you would have $100,000 in options, and $100,000 in CASH. LEAPS are very volatile so we always put 50% of our investment in LEAPS and 50% in CASH. This doesn't have to be exactly 50% (it can't be) because you can only buy and sell contracts (100 options) – not individual options. But it should be pretty close.

One disadvantage nowadays of keeping a great amount of cash in your broker's money market account, is that Money Market accounts pay a very low interest rate. For many years it has been less than 1% which means you're not earning very much on the money. But having cash to buy shares at cheaper prices is an essential feature that will pay off for you later on when your stock or other investment goes down and you need to buy more shares.

Side note and BONUS TIP: I have found a way you can make high interest on your CASH balance – put your CASH money into High-Yielding REITS like AGNC or NLY which pays a monthly dividend. In 2018 some REITS paid more than 12% dividend per year. There are other good REITS and high yielding closed-end funds also where you can keep part of your cash and earn high interest. I could write an entire chapter on good REITS for your AIM cash. If you search the blog on my website (www.jjjinvesting.biz) you will find an article where I list a lot of my favorites. As one of my clients you will get my latest knowledge and recommendations.

Your CASH total will go up or down every month depending on whether you're buying and selling and earning interest on your cash. Also I view it as optional if you want to deduct the cost of the commissions as you make buys and sells. Personally I wouldn't bother worrying about the commissions; you make enough profits without really worrying about it.

You'll see that the AIM method is very conservative as half of your investment will go to CASH. If you have a buy, then Column 6 (CASH) − Column 11 (MARKET ORDER BUY) X 1.005 (interest) equals next month's cash total. When you have a sell, Column 6 CASH + Column 11 MARKER ORDER (SELL) x 1.005 equals next month's cash total.

Column 7 – LEAPS CONTRACTS BOUGHT (SOLD) - After you receive notification that you have had a buy or sell from your brokerage account, find out what the details were after the market closes for the day. And be sure to check on a consistent basis! You might be buying some options, selling some options, or doing nothing. In this column you will record the number of long-term options (LEAPS) contracts you bought or sold for that particular day. If you did nothing, put − (dash) in the column. To arrive at the number of option contracts you bought or sold, you divide the dollar amount in column 11 (MARKET ORDER BOUGHT (SOLD) by the option LEAPS PRICE in column 3. For example, if AIM tells you to sell 3 contracts (300 options) and the LEAPS contracts are selling for $3,500, then you sell 3 contracts for $10,500. Remember to put the ( ) around the sold contracts to keep separate the buy and sell transactions which are sharing the same column.

Column 8 – LEAPS OWNED - This is the number of option shares you currently own. This figure will constantly go up and down. Column 8 equals last month's column 8 plus any option contracts you bought in the previous month. If you sold any option contracts you would subtract the number sold from previous month's total to see your current number of contracts. If the previous day that you did AIM and AIM told you don't need to make any buys or sells; then column 8 would be the same number of option shares in the row just above the current row you're using.

Column 9 PORTFOLIO CONTROL – This is another important column. When you start, put a control amount equal to the dollar amount of option contracts you bought to start (this is only a control number, no money involved with this column.) If you start with $100,000 worth of options, your PORTFOLIO CONTROL number is also 100,000. After your initial injection of money, PORTFOLIO CONTROL will only change if you buy more options. Every time you buy more, you <u>add half the amount you bought</u> to your PORTFOLIO CONTROL total. For example, AIM tells you to buy $80,000 worth of option contracts; you add $40,000 to your prior PORTFOLIO CONTROL total. If no buy, then column 9 is the same as the prior month. I explain more about this rationale elsewhere in the book.

Column 10 – BUY (SELL) ADVICE - Every month you look at your option LEAPS VALUE (column 4) and PORTFOLIO CONTROL. If your option LEAPS VALUE is higher, you put that figure on top. If your PORTFOLIO CONTROL amount is higher, you put that on top. For example: if your option LEAPS VALUE is $100,000 and your PORTFOLIO CONTROL amount is $70,000 you put LEAPS VALUE on top. Like this:

LEAPS VALUE	$100,000
- PORTFOLIO CONTROL	70,000
= (SELL) ADVICE	$30,000

Or if PORTFOLIO CONTROL is higher (with other numbers as examples):

PORTFOLIO CONTROL	$125,000
- LEAPS VALUE	$75,000
= BUY ADVICE	$50,000

Hopefully the bottom line as a buy or sell makes sense to you here but if not I'll explain it. When your LEAPS VALUE is higher than your PORTFOLIO CONTROL it means your LEAPS is heading in the direction of a SELL. When your LEAPS VALUE is lower, it means you are heading in the direction of a BUY. You always want to BUY LOW and SELL HIGH! Those directions explain the relation between your LEAPS VALUE and your PORTFOLIO CONTROL.

Column 11 – MARKET ORDER BUY (SELL) - This is the column that tells you whether you execute an order with your stockbroker or not. You take the amount from column 10, BUY (SELL) ADVICE, and subtract out the SAFE (column 5) amount. Look at whether the amount is over the value of two contracts.

If the difference is more than the value of two LEAPS contracts, you have exceeded the threshold for a buy or sell according to AIM. Depending on the LEAPS price, since you pay a commission for every buy or sell, you want to see a difference large enough for 2, maybe 3 contracts. Then the commissions are a much smaller fraction of the trade. With FAANGS and FAANG-Like LEAPS selling or buying at least 2 contracts every time will greatly increase your profits!

When you have your number of contracts to buy or sell you go online and use the limit buys and sells to make the trades happen automatically. If you have a sell order, you have to figure out how many option contracts you must sell (column 11 divided by column 3, LEAPS PRICE X 100) and tell your broker (or set your brokerage account) to sell that many contracts. For example, if your market order was to sell $30,000 worth of $10,000 option contract, then you would tell your broker to sell 3 contracts. You would do the same exact thing if it's a buy order, you divide the dollar amount of the buy order by the current price of the option and that determines how many contracts you buy. Always remember investing is both an art and a science, so if the AIM strategy tells you to buy 2.7 contracts, then you can easily round that off to buy 3 contracts and everything will work fine.

COLUMN 12 – 6% INTEREST - This is the amount of interest earned by your cash total from column 6. The .005 is 1/12 of 6% or the amount of interest you earn in one month. I picked 6% because it's easy to work with over of time and is a fair average of the interest rate you can earn on REITS and high-yield closed-end funds over the long-term and it keeps things simple – monthly interest is always one half of 1%. Remember we are in this for the long haul and if you play AIM over the next 20-30 years, your REITS and high-yield closed-end funds will average out to 6% interest over the years. I can help you to earn the 6% by buying REITS and High Yield Closed-End funds that pay 6% or higher with your Cash if you ask for my help.

COLUMN 13 - # of CONTRACTS OWNED - This is the number of LEAPS owned in Col. 8 divided by 100. For example 800 options divided by 100 = 8 contracts.

Column 14 – PORTFOLIO VALUE - Add the value of your CASH (column 6) + LEAPS VALUE (column 4), the value of your long-term options (LEAPS) and you have the total current value of your investment. You will notice one nice thing about the AIM spreadsheet. Once you start with the LEAPS you see exactly what you're starting amount is in the very first row when you look at PORTFOLIO VALUE. In this example we are starting with a PORTFOLIO VALUE of $301,537. And then in future months you can see how much you are ahead in profits!

So when you compare PORTFOLIO VALUE in the future rows, you can easily see exactly what your status is. If the PORTFOLIO VALUE is higher than the beginning PORTFOLIO VALUE $301,537 then you are ahead or profitable. If the PORTFOLIO VALUE is less than $301,537, you currently have a "paper loss." All that means is that the option or other investment is cheaper than when you originally bought it, and possibly AIM is telling you to buy more option shares of this cheap option so when it turns around and goes higher later on you will own more option shares that will go up in value and that will increase your profits.

GOING THROUGH AN EXAMPLE WITH AIM

Now I will go through an actual LEAPS buy or sell and show you just how easy it is. Get your pencil, calculator, and 14–column paper or your printed Excel spreadsheet. I can email you blank AIM LEAPS spreadsheets to use if you ask me. Write all the headings in the proper columns. Now write the symbol of the company. Then write the date and strike price for the LEAPS. Here you will see AMZN Jan 2020 S 1200. S is for strike price.

For this example I picked Amazon (AMZN). See the complete spreadsheet at the end of this Chapter. The first month in our example is December 2017 (12/17); write that in your date column. Then we are going to imagine that we start with $301,537 to invest. This is the amount we rolled over from the end of the 2nd year.

Having a calculator will make your figuring easier. We are going to start with December 2017 because that is an example. The numbers would be different today of course but the process is the same. With LEAPS you must select a Strike Price and an option year. We will always use the latest LEAPS we can buy which rollover in December.

The first month is Dec 17 (12/17), write that in your date column. Then we are going to imagine that we are starting with $301,537 to invest. This happens to be the actual number after starting with $100,000 two years earlier.

DECEMBER 2017

We start with $301,537 after tripling our original $100,000 from 2 years ago to invest. First we look up the **theoretical price** of the long-term option (LEAPS) from the stock broker or on broker's website or app. All you have to do is type in the symbol and you'll see exactly what the current price of any stock or options is. When you actually buy your stock or option, you'll be able to go your account online and see what price you paid. For original buy price we will use a limit price so we know what price we paid. **Remember to be careful you are checking the right options year and Strike Price!**

LEAPS prices and some stock prices can move quickly so you want to place an online Limit order to buy Amazon. Suppose your brokerage account says the Last Price is $190.25. You also see the LEAPS had a Theoretical Price of $195.70. We <u>always use the theoretical price</u> (the average of bid and ask price) because it's the most accurate at any given time. Write that in column 3. For a Theoretical Price of $195.70 I would recommend a Limit Buy price of $190.00

Our first LEAPS value will be about half the starting amount for the third year, rounding off to whole contracts. With LEAPS we always go 50% LEAPS, 50% Cash. Write $156,560 in Col. 4 – we got that number by multiplying one option's value ($195.70 X 800 options or 8 contracts as contracts contain 100 options.

Then in column 5, write $15,656 because SAFE Value is always 10% of the LEAPS VALUE. Then write $144,977 in column 6 because it's your remaining cash after taking the original Portfolio Total of $301,537 - LEAPS VALUE $156,560 = $144,977. In column 8 you write the number of shares you own. This is figured by dividing LEAPS VALUE in column 4 by the LEAPS PRICE – in column 3 - $156,560 divided by $195.70 equals 800 options. I haven't shown column 5 in the book for the sake of making more space for the other columns.

Column 10 doesn't come into play yet, and column 11 doesn't either. Column 12 is blank also. Now add up the value of the LEAPS you bought in column 4 and the amount of CASH in column 6 and you have your total for PORTFOLIO VALUE. Add $156,560 LEAPS VALUE+ $144,977 CASH equals $301,537.

Now let me show you how simple and profitable the method will be for you. Remember to reinvest some of your cash into REITS or closed-end high yield funds. Just tell your broker when you open your account that you always want any dividends placed into your money market account and you do not want to buy additional shares or fractions of shares with any dividends you receive. **Long-term options (LEAPS) do not pay dividends on options – only your REITS or closed-end funds pay dividends.**

JANUARY 2018

Date Col. 1	Remarks Col. 2 AMZN 2020 S 1200	LEAPS Price Col. 3	LEAPS Value Col .4	Cash Col. 6	Con-Tracts Bought (Sold) Col. 7	LEAPS Owned Col. 8	Port-Folio Control Col. 9	Buy (Sell) Advice Col. 10	Market Order (Sell) Buy Col. 11	# Of Con-tracts Col. 13	Port-Folio Value Col. 14
12/17		195.70	156560	144977	-`	800	156560	-	-	8	301,537
1/18	Ignore Sell	234.50	187600	145847	-	800	156560	(31040)	(12280)	8	333,447

Here is how we use AIM in the real world. Jan 1 - you look up the **theoretical price** of the AMZN Jan 2020 Strike 1200 Call. And it's $234.50, up nicely.

Today everything you want is either on a website or your iPhone on your iPad etc. so now on we would just say we look it up on the web. My new iPhone has this great little feature; all I have to do is press the TD Ameritrade app on the very opening screen and I can find out all the information on stock or LEAPS prices you ever dreamed of.

We find Amazon and see that the price for Jan is $234.50, which we write in column 3. Did you remember to put Jan '18 - 1/18 - in the date column? Now go to column 8 for Jan '18. Look above in column 8 and you will see you owned 800 options in Dec '17. You didn't buy or sell any in column 7. This is why you leave column 7 blank in the first month. You still own 800 options. Write 800 in column 8 for Jan '18.

Also your PORTFOLIO CONTROL amount is still the same (you didn't buy anything in addition to the opening buy in the first month, when you opened your account), so write 156,560 in column 9. Now multiply the number of shares owned (800) by the options price ($234.50) and you have your LEAPS VALUE for column 4. Now CASH, you'll notice, has grown from $144,977 to $145,847. This is because you earned $870 interest ($144,977 X .005) which you write in column 12. If you had bought or sold LEAPS the preceding month, would have also affected cash this month. I hid column 12 in the book to make more space for other columns.

Now you take your two key amounts – LEAPS VALUE and PORTFOLIO CONTROL and look at them. Which is higher? LEAPS VALUE is higher ($187,600) than PORTFOLIO

CONTROL ($156,560). Since LEAPS VALUE is higher, put LEAPS VALUE on top. You'll be seeing this chart every month. Once you start doing this, you won't need the chart, but it's a good way to learn.

LEAPS VALUE	$187,600
- PORTFOLIO CONTROL	$156,560
= (SELL) ADVICE	$(31,040)
- SAFE Value	$18,760
= MARKET ORDER (SELL)	$(12,280)

You now have a potential SELL for ($12,280) but it's only potential. Now look at the SAFE amount in column 5 and you find that it is $18,760 which is higher than your MARKET SELL advice in column 11.

The purpose of the SAFE amount is to set a threshold or buffer for your trading. Whenever the difference between your LEAPS VALUE and PORTFOLIO CONTROL is less than your SAFE amount (whether positive or negative) it means you are "SAFE" to do nothing!

So you put Ignore (12,280) in column 11, MARKET ORDER (SELL) because your signal isn't strong enough to give you a market order yet. Put a "–"(dash) in column 7 since you won't be buying or selling any LEAPS this month. Be patient, AIM doesn't want you to sell or buy too soon. You'll get plenty of chances.

Now all you have to do is figure column 14, PORTFOLIO VALUE. You remember, add column 4, LEAPS VALUE and column 6, CASH and you have the current value of your investment. This month it's $187,600 + $145,847 = $333,447. If the LEAPS goes up in price, you'll have a potential sell and if it goes down, a potential buy.

Here is Feb '18. I'll be shorter in my explanations and you'll see you will still understand because you did the same thing every month. While every month is done the same, the outcome can be quite different.

February 2018

Date Col. 1	Remarks Col. 2 AMZN 2020 S 1200	LEAPS Price Col. 3	LEAPS Value Col .4	Cash Col. 6	Con-tracts Bought (Sold) Col. 7	LEAPS Owned Col. 8	Portfolio Control Col. 9	Buy (Sell) Advice Col. 10	Market Order (Sell) Buy Col. 11	# Of Con-tracts Col. 13	Portfolio Value Col. 14
1/18		234.50	187600	145847	-`	800	156560	(31040)	(12280)	8	333,447
2/18		358.43	286744	146721	(4)	800	156560	(130184)	(143372)	8	433,465

First look up the price of Amazon's LEAPS. Jan 2020 Strike 1200 Call LEAPS price is $358.43. Write that in column 3. Then multiply the number of shares owned (still 800 LEAPS since you didn't buy or sell any last month) by the price of one option and that gives you a LEAPS VALUE of $286,744. SAFE is always 10% so write 28,674 in column 5. Again the only thing that affected CASH is INTEREST; you earned $874. So write $874 in column 12 (hidden here) and add $874 to your CASH. You now have $146,721 in CASH. Since you didn't buy any LEAPS last month, PORTFOLIO CONTROL stays the same at 156,560.

The magic two numbers are LEAPS VALUE and PORTFOLIO CONTROL. Again, since LEAPS VALUE is higher, put that on top. Since LEAPS VALUE is higher, you have a potential (sell) signal:

LEAPS VALUE	$286,744 (Col. 4)
- PORTFOLIO CONTROL	$156,560 (Col. 9)
= (SELL) ADVICE	$(130184) (Col. 10)
Now subtract SAFE from (SELL) ADVICE	- 28,674 (Col. 5)
= MARKET ORDER (SELL) - RECOMMENDED	$(101,510) (Col. 11)
= MARKET ORDER (SELL) - ACTUAL	$(143,372) (Col. 11)

We did something different here. The math gives you a (SELL) MARKER ORDER of $101,510. But I decided to increase the sell from 2.83 contracts to four because the gain was so high for February. That results in the actual (SELL) MARKET ORDER of

$143,372. AIM is also an Art – not just a Science!

You should be writing all these figures on your sample spreadsheet the same as the illustration at the end of the Chapter shows.

As you can see, you're getting your first sell order. Now divide $143,372 by the PRICE ($358.48) and you have 400 options to sell. Write (4) in CONTRACTS BOUGHT (SOLD) column. Remember there are 100 options in every contract and it is contracts that you trade.

Now finish your month's work by figuring out your PORTFOLIO VALUE. It's LEAPS VALUE ($286,744) + column 6 CASH ($148,721) = $433,465 PORTFOLIO VALUE Col. 14. Now you go to your online trading account and execute a sell for 4 contracts of Amazon 2020 Strike 1200 Call.

You're ahead $131,928 since December 2017. But better things are still ahead.

Now let's go even quicker because I'm sure you understand how simple and repetitive the method is and soon you'll see its power. Try doing the next month on your own. Remember to start by looking up the price of Amazon. Since this is an example in the past I'll tell you the "new" price. Soon you'll be doing your own stocks and this will be the first step.

March 2018

Date Col. 1	Remarks Col. 2 AMZN 2020 S 1200	LEAPS Price Col. 3	LEAPS Value Col .4	Cash Col. 6	Contracts Bought (Sold) Col. 7	LEAPS Owned Col. 8	Portfolio Control Col. 9	Buy (Sell) Advice Col. 10	Market Order (Sell) Buy Col. 11	# Of Contracts Col. 13	Portfolio Value Col. 14
2/18		358.43	286744	146721	(4)`	800	156560	(130184)	(143372)	8	433,465
3/18	Ignore Sell	516.00	206400	291543	-	400	156560	(49840)	(29200)	4	497,943

Okay, the price has risen and is now $516.00. If you want to, take a break here and try to update the spreadsheet yourself. Next I will explain the steps.

Write down $516.00 and then fill in column 9 that didn't change since no buying last month. But column 8, LEAPS OWNED, did change. We sold 4 contracts last month. So subtract 4 contracts from the column 8 total from the prior month (800 - 400 = 400). Write 400 in column 8, LEAPS OWNED. Now figure column 6 CASH. You started with $146.721 and must add the $143,372 you got from selling the LEAPS. So $146,721+ $143,372 = $290,093 + $1450 for INTEREST = $291,543. WRITE that in column 6, CASH. Write $1,450 in column 12, INTEREST.

Then compare column 4 with column 9 and see which is higher. LEAPS VALUE is still higher $206,400 To PORTFOLIO CONTROL's 156,560. You can figure you have a potential (SELL) of $49,840 that you write in column 10. You compare to SAFE (10% of the LEAPS VALUE) and see its lower than your potential (SELL) ADVICE so you subtract SAFE from the difference: 49,840 - 20,640 = 29,200. You write (29,200) in column 11, MARKET ORDER (SELL) BUY.

Do you actually have a sell? No you don't because the cost of one contract is $51,600 and you only have a MARKET SELL for $29,200; about half the price of one contract.

Remember it's CASH + LEAPS VALUE = PORTFOLIO VALUE which is $497,943 for this month.

April 2018

Date Col. 1	Remarks Col. 2 AMZN 2020 S 1200	LEAPS Price Col. 3	LEAPS Value Col .4	Cash Col. 6	Contracts Bought (Sold) Col. 7	LEAPS Owned Col. 8	Portfolio Control Col. 9	Buy (Sell) Advice Col. 10	Market Order (Sell) Buy Col. 11	# Of Contracts Col. 13	Portfolio Value Col. 14
3/18	Ignore	516.00	206400	291543	-	400	156560	(49840)	(29200)	4	497,943
4/18		383.00	153200	293000	-	400	156560	3360	-	4	446,200

Now it's April 2018. LEAPS price dropped to $383.00. Again write the LEAPS OWNED and PORTFOLIO CONTROL numbers in columns 8 and 9. Column 9, PORTFOLIO CONTROL hasn't changed since last month because no buying and LEAPS OWNED did not change since we did no buying or selling. So go to last month's column 8 total and copy the same number 400 in Col. 8 and write that number in column 8. Now figure LEAPS VALUE $153,200 (Col.3 X Col.8) and you see it's less than $156,560 PORTFOLIO CONTROL. SAFE is always 10% of LEAPS VALUE so fill that in. CASH again was affected by interest. You started with $291,543 and added $1,457 INTEREST = $293,000.

Now look at PORTFOLIO CONTROL and it is higher than LEAPS VALUE so put PORTFOLIO CONTROL on top. Think P for purchase. You have BUY ADVICE of $3,360. Before you do anything, you still must compare BUY ADVICE to SAFE. SAFE is going to cancel this market order because it is greater than the BUY ADVICE.

I just use a − symbol when I do nothing. Again if you haven't given yourself $1,457 in INTEREST, add $1,457 to your CASH account and again add LEAPS VALUE and CASH to obtain your PORTFOLIO VALUE. Your PORTFOLIO VALUE is $446,200, down a little for April '18.

May 2018

Date Col. 1	Remarks Col. 2 AMZN 2020 S 1200	LEAPS Price Col. 3	LEAPS Value Col .4	Cash Col. 6	Contracts Bought (Sold) Col. 7	LEAPS Owned Col. 8	Portfolio Control Col. 9	Buy (Sell) Advice Col. 10	Market Order (Sell) Buy Col. 11	# Of Contracts Col. 13	Portfolio Value Col. 14
4/18		383.00	153200	293000	-	400	156560	3360	-	4	446,200
5/18		519.50	207800	294464	(1)	400	156560	(51240)	(51950)	4	502,264

Now it's May 2018 and the LEAPS have risen a lot! Remember the beauty of the strategy: buy low and sell high. Watch it work. LEAPS PRICE has risen to $519.50. Write it in LEAPS PRICE and number of LEAPS OWNED and PORTFOLIO CONTROL, which didn't change since no buying last month. Now multiply number of options (400) X LEAPS PRICE $519.50 and your LEAPS VALUE is $207,800. Again SAFE is 10% of LEAPS VALUE or 20,780. CASH has earned another $1,464 of INTEREST, write that in column 12 and add the $1,464 to CASH total in column 6. Look at LEAPS VALUE and PORTFOLIO CONTROL and as you thought, LEAPS VALUE is higher which could possibly signal a sell. Write LEAPS VALUE on top and PORTFOLIO CONTROL below as shown here:

LEAPS VALUE	$207,800
- PORTFOLIO CONTROL	156,560
= (SELL) ADVICE	$51,240

Now compare your (SELL) ADVICE to SAFE and you see that SAFE overrules any selling this month by strict AIM rules because one contract is worth $51,950 which is higher than the (sell) advice price to buy even one contract at $51,240. However I notice that Amazon LEAPS are extremely expensive and we only have 4 contracts – so I overrule the SAFE amount and decide to sell one contract for a very good profit. AIM is not set in stone so use common sense every so often to do what's best for you!

You can also see that AIM isn't as easy or profitable to do with just a few contracts. When one contract price is a small fraction of your LEAPS VALUE you will find more opportunities to buy and sell your contracts.

The MARKET ORDER (SELL) is $51,950. Again finish off the month by figuring your LEAPS VALUE + CASH or $207,800 + $294,464 = $502,264 or your investment is up $200,727 since the beginning. Keep thinking long-term.

June 2018

Date Col. 1	Remarks Col. 2 AMZN 2020 S 1200	LEAPS Price Col. 3	LEAPS Value Col .4	Cash Col. 6	Contracts Bought (Sold) Col. 7	LEAPS Owned Col. 8	Portfolio Control Col. 9	Buy (Sell) Advice Col. 10	Market Order (Sell) Buy Col. 11	# Of Contracts Col. 13	Portfolio Value Col. 14
5/18		519.50	207800	294464	(1)	400	156560	(51240)	(51950)	4	502,264
6/18	Ignore Sell	590.00	177000	348146	-	300	156560	(20440)	(2740)	3	525,146

Now we are in June 2018. Again look up the LEAPS PRICE, it's $590.00. Write it in column 3. Now go to column 8, LEAPS OWNED and column 9, PORTFOLIO CONTROL; since you did nothing last month both stayed the same. Now continue business as usual.

Since you sold one contract (100 options), you now have 300 shares remaining. Multiply the number of LEAPS (300) X LEAPS PRICE $590.00) and your LEAPS VALUE is $177,000. Write it in column 4. SAFE is 10% of LEAPS VALUE so write in 17,700. CASH was affected by your sell on one contract ($51,950) and affected by INTEREST so add $1,732 to this month's total. Write in $348,146 in column 6 and write $1,732 in column 12, INTEREST. Now compare PORTFOLIO CONTROL to LEAPS VALUE. LEAPS VALUE is $177,000 and bigger than PORTFOLIO CONTROL so you place it on top. Again remember P for purchase if PORTFOLIO CONTROL is on top and S for sell if LEAPS VALUE is on top. AIM is very simple. So do your calculations:

LEAPS VALUE	$177,000
- PORTFOLIO CONTROL	156,560
= (SELL) ADVICE	$20,440
- SAFE	17,700
= MARKET (SELL) ORDER	$ (2,740)

You do nothing – no selling because SELL amount is too low. Then you figure PORTFOLIO VALUE. Remember how? See this is easy. You added LEAPS VALUE of $177,000 + CASH of $348,146 = $525,146. You're ahead $223,609 since December 2017.

July 2018

Date Col. 1	Remarks Col. 2 AMZN 2020 S 1200	LEAPS Price Col. 3	LEAPS Value Col .4	Cash Col. 6	Contracts Bought (Sold) Col. 7	LEAPS Owned Col. 8	Portfolio Control Col. 9	Buy (Sell) Advice Col. 10	Market Order (Sell) Buy Col. 11	# Of Contracts Col. 13	Portfolio Value Col. 14
6/18		590.00	177000	348146	-	300	156560	(20440)	(2947)	3	525,146
7/18		622.50	186750	349887	1	300	156560	-	-	3	536,637
7/18	Adjust L/C	622.50	249000	287637	-	400	249000	-	-	4	536,637

Now here is something different that will help you make even more profits. I discovered this trick myself. When you have lots of selling the 50-50% ratio between CASH and LEAPS Value gets distorted. Look above at July 2018 and you see the LEAPS is $186,750 and the CASH total is $349,887 – way out of whack. So I decided to adjust the LEAPS/CASH balance. Take your PORTFOLIO TOTAL of $536,637 and divide by 2 = $268,319. Next divide $268,319 by the LEAPS Contract price of $62,250 = 4.3 contracts. So we buy one more contract. We make our profits from having LEAPS go up – not interest on large cash balances. When you rebalance CASH and LEAPS Value you must change the PORTFOLIO CONTROL amount to the new LEAPS VALUE of $249,000 and then there is no buying or selling for that month. In effect you did buy one more contract.

August 2018

Date Col. 1	Remarks Col. 2 AMZN 2020 S 1200	LEAPS Price Col. 3	LEAPS Value Col .4	Cash Col. 6	Contracts Bought (Sold) Col. 7	LEAPS Owned Col. 8	Portfolio Control Col. 9	Buy (Sell) Advice Col. 10	Market Order (Sell) Buy Col. 11	# Of Contracts Col. 13	Portfolio Value Col. 14
7/18	Adjust L/C	622.30	249000	287637	1	400	249000	-	-	4	536,637
8/18	Ignore Sell	784.01	313604	289389	(1)	400	249000	(64604)	(78401)	3	602,993

On to August '18. The explanations are becoming shorter because you're getting smarter and seeing how easy this is. The LEAPS PRICE rose to $784.01 a share. Write it down and then do columns 8 and 9. Column 8, LEAPS OWNED, will stay the same since we adjusted the LEAPS/Cash balance back to 50-50 Cash & LEAPS last month. Cash grows by the interest earned so $1,752 + 287,637 = 289,389. Column 9, PORTFOLIO CONTROL stays the same since there was no buying last month.

LEAPS VALUE is 400 options X $784.01 = $313,604. SAFE is always 10% of LEAPS VALUE so SAFE is 31,360. CASH was affected by re-adjusting our stock/cash ratio. We find that LEAPS Value is higher than PORTFOLIO CONTROL:

LEAPS VALUE	$313,604
- PORTFOLIO CONTOL	249,000
= (SELL) ADVICE	($64,604)
- SAFE	31,360
= MARKET (SELL) ORDER	($78,401)

You have a (SELL) MARKET ORDER because AIM is an art and not a science. You only own 4 contracts because Amazon is so expensive. Your (Sell) Advise is $64,604. Your LEAPS went from $622.30 to $784.01, about a $160.00 jump. I felt happy taking profits by selling one contract at this high price.

September 2018

Date Col. 1	Remarks Col. 2 AMZN 2020 S 1200	LEAPS Price Col. 3	LEAPS Value Col .4	Cash Col. 6	Contracts Bought (Sold) Col. 7	LEAPS Owned Col. 8	Portfolio Control Col. 9	Buy (Sell) Advice Col. 10	Market Order (Sell) Buy Col. 11	# Of Contracts Col. 13	Portfolio Value Col. 14
8/18	Ignore Sell	784.01	313604	289389	(1)	400	249000	(64604)	(78401)	4	602,993
9/18	Ignore Sell	855.00	256500	369629	-	300	249000	(7500)	-	4	626,129

Now September. The LEAPS PRICE is up to $85,500, up $7,100.01 from last month. Go to columns 8 and 9. You SOLD one LEAPS contract last month so CONTRACTS OWNED drops to 3 contracts. PORTFOLIO CONTROL stays the same since we did not buy last month. Write these two numbers in. LEAPS VALUE is 300 X $855.00 equals $256,500. SAFE is 25,650. CASH is $289,389 + $78,401 SELL + $1,839 INTEREST = $626,129. Again compare PORTFOLIO CONTROL and LEAPS VALUE and LEAPS

VALUE is slightly higher. Do your calculations:

LEAPS VALUE	$256,500
- PORTFOLIO CONTROL	249,000
= (SELL) ADVICE	($7,500)
- SAFE	25,650
= DO NOTHING	$0

All that's left is to figure is PORTFOLIO VALUE. It's $256,500 LEAPS + $369,629 Cash = $626,129.

Using this example that is a real data of LEAPS on Amazon, **you would be ahead 108% from December 2017 to September 2018 in ten months.**

Robert Lichello first created AIM as a method to trade individual stocks. It made him a millionaire. You can still use AIM for stocks but the example you saw here was with LEAPS. From reading the earlier chapters you know that once you have a system like AIM you'll want to use it with investments that have more leverage and volatility than stocks. LEAPS are options on the same company's stocks so you are getting more benefits from AIM without any additional risk.

Study this example and you'll see how you made your profit. Your portfolio went consistently up for 10 months. Buy low and sell high shouldn't only be a cliché. It should be - and is - put into practice through the Automatic Investment Management method. AIM produces the results you want from an investment.

There is one essential part of AIM I haven't explained yet and that is the Automatic part. This example required you to check your prices every month. That is hardly a big time commitment compared to day traders but it is still something. It is also reactive.

Once a month is an arbitrary frequency to use. I use it in the "model" portfolios in my newsletter. But once you actually own LEAPs I strongly recommend you check them every market day after the market closes. Better yet - create your system that checks every day for you - automatically. That will be covered in the next chapter. What if the price changes enough for a trade in the middle of the month and then it has reversed again by the end of the month? You would have missed your chance for the trade.

Knowing how to calculate your minimum buy and sell amounts ahead of time - and then setting up these trades to happen automatically the moment they are ready - is the next powerful feature of AIM.

CHAPTER 7

How to Trade Automatically With AIM

By now you should know when you see a new LEAPS price whether or not a trade is required. But how can you calculate the right price <u>ahead of time</u> and have your account ready to "pull the trigger" on the trade - automatically?

You trade automatically by setting up Limit Buys and Limit Sells with your stock broker. When you go to the broker's buy and sell screen (see illustrations later in this chapter) you tell your broker what price you are willing to buy or sell at.

What *is* the RIGHT price to <u>scientifically</u> and <u>systematically</u> buy low or sell high?

This is the magic question that investors have been asking for decades. Actually hundreds of years! Maybe thousands!

Thanks to Robert Lichello who first invented the AIM method, there is a way to find the answer.

Thanks to the 30+ years I have been successful using his strategy and more recently applying it to long-term options (LEAPS), I'm going to show you how it's done.

Thanks to the amazing tools today we have with the internet and online trading, you can automate this even more than Robert Lichello could have imagined when he first created AIM.

Let's return to a previous example. First you have to learn how to calculate the future buy and sell prices where you want to make a trade. Here is the first month of our example with AMZN.

JANUARY 2018 - TABLE 1

Date Col. 1	Remarks Col. 2 AMZN 2020 S 1200	LEAPS Price Col. 3	LEAPS Value Col .4	Cash Col. 6	Contracts Bought (Sold) Col. 7	LEAPS Owned Col. 8	Portfolio Control Col. 9	Buy (Sell) Advice Col. 10	Market Order (Sell) Buy Col. 11	# Of Contracts Col. 13	Portfolio Value Col. 14
12/17		195.70	156560	144977	-`	800	156560	-	-	8	301,537
1/18	Ignore Sell	234.50	187600	145847	-	800	156560	(31040)	(12280)	8	333,447
Buy	4 Contracts	125.00	100000			800	156560	56560	46560	8	
Sell	3 Contracts	350.00	280000			800	156560	(123440)	(95440)	8	

Here's how I calculate the buy and sell calculations. Both math and judgment play a part.

Owning only 8 contracts means the buy will be lower and the sell price higher than if we owned the ideal number of contracts (a minimum of 15). AIM will do the correct math whether we own 8 or 15 so you will always get the right amount.

Next we want a buy and sell price that let us <u>buy or sell at least 2 contracts, preferably 4 contracts</u>. I don't recommend just buying or selling one contract – you'll pay too much in commissions and lower your profits.

Here is the math: I found from experience that the buy price will be about 40% lower than the current price. So first I tried a buy price of $150.00 an option and found it wasn't low enough to let me buy four contracts. I keep it simple by using round numbers – so next I tried $125.00. I found that $125.00 was the right amount to buy 4 contracts – I went with a lower amount to buy more contracts and be a little bearish in this current market. You see why I do calculations in pencil with a big eraser!

Here are the actual buy calculations. You want to calculate the difference between the Portfolio Control and the new LEAPS Value. Portfolio Control will be higher **because you deliberately chose a buy price about 40% lower than original buy price.** Then you want to calculate a SAFE value of 10% of the LEAPS Value **because you always subtract 10% from your buy advice before having a buy market order.** Then you subtract the SAFE value from your buy advice because AIM wants you to hold back on buying. If the trends continue you saved some of your money to buy at an even lower price. The final answer is total value of LEAPS you want to buy. You'll then need to divide this number by the number of contracts you want to trade. It doesn't have to be an exact match but it should be close.

Here is the buy process one step at a time.

What is your Portfolio Control? It is $156,560. This is the same as your original buy Portfolio Control.

Guess - what is the LEAPS value that would decrease enough to justify a Buy? From experience it will be at least 40% less. To start, I tried $150.00, and then $125.00 and $125.00 worked to buy 4 contracts.

Take Portfolio Control $156,560 minus LEAPS Value $100,000 = $56,560. This is your Buy Advice.

What is the Buy Advice? It is the difference between these two numbers or $56,560.

Next calculate the SAFE Value. It is 10% of your new LEAPS Value. 10% of $100,000 is $10,000.

Subtract your SAFE Value from the Buy Advice. This lowers your Market Order to $46,560.

The last step is to calculate how many contracts "fit" within this value. Take $46,560 divided by $10,000 (the cost of one contract - remember you have 100 LEAPS per contract). That means $46,450 gives you enough money to buy 4 contracts (actually 3.7 contracts rounded up) or 400 options.

Here is the math for a Sell. I found from experience that the sell price will be about 40% higher than the original price or the current price after a previous buy or sell. So first I tried a Sell price of $300.00 an option. I will spare you some time and tell you that I found it wasn't high enough to let me buy two contracts. I keep it simple by using round numbers – so finally I tried $350.00. You see why I do calculations in pencil with a big eraser!

Here are the actual sell calculations. You want to calculate the difference between the new LEAPS value and the Portfolio Control value. LEAPS will be higher because you arbitrarily chose a price higher than your initial buy. Then you want to calculate a SAFE value of 10% of the LEAPS Value because you always subtract SAFE amount from limit Sell advice and the new total is your Limit sell market order. You subtract the SAFE value because AIM wants you to hold back on selling. If next month your LEAPS are higher (trends tend to continue) you made even more profit by selling at an even higher price. The final answer is the total value of LEAPS you want to buy. You'll then need to divide this number by the number of contracts you want to trade. It doesn't have to be exact match but it should be close.

Here is the sell process one step at a time.

What is your Portfolio Control? It is $156,560. It is the same as your original buy Portfolio Control.

Guess - what is the LEAPS value that would increase enough to justify a Sell? From experience it will be at least 40% more. To start I tried $325.00, and then $350.00. I found that $350.00 worked to sell 3 contracts. You'll see below we use $280,000 – not $350.00. That's because we need the total value of all 800 options (LEAPS) we own - $350.00 X 800 = $280,000.

Take LEAPS Value $280,000 minus Portfolio Control $156,560 = Sell Advice $123,440.

What is the Sell Advice? It is the difference between these two numbers or $123,440.

Next calculate the SAFE Value. It is 10% of your new LEAPS Value so 10% of $280,000 is $28,000.

Subtract your SAFE Value from the Sell Advice. This lowers your Market Order to $95,440. You are left with $95,440 to sell.

The last step is to calculate how many contracts "fit" within this value. If 2 contracts is enough for a Sell then take $95,440 divided by $35,000 (the cost of one contract - remember you have 100 LEAPS per contract). So $95,440 gives you enough money to sell 3 contracts or 300 options. The actual math is $95,440 divided by $35,000 = sell 2.73 contracts but that is close enough to 3 contracts so we round that up.

You want to put the above buy and sell information on the bottom of your spreadsheet. Here is the result:

TABLE 2

Date Col. 1	Remarks Col. 2 AMZN 2020 S 1200	LEAPS Price Col. 3	LEAPS Value Col .4	Cash Col. 6	Contracts Bought (Sold) Col. 7	LEAPS Owned Col. 8	Portfolio Control Col. 9	Buy (Sell) Advice Col. 10	Market Order (Sell) Buy Col. 11	Portfolio Value Col. 12
Buy	4 Contracts	125.00	100000			800	156560	56560	46360	
Sell	3 Contracts	350.00	280000			800	156560	(123440)	(95440)	

Now the above calculations were a combination of Lichello's method where he always uses 10% SAFE for buys and sells and my judgment. Always remember AIM is both an art and a science – you're not trying to figure the value of Pi out to a million decimal places – just two or three.

In the above example Robert Lichello and I would agree with the buy and sell prices because you could use the 10% SAFE amount to subtract from Buy and (Sell) Advice. But when you are in a Bear Market you would run out of Cash too quickly before the LEAPS' price hit bottom and started rising.

That is when you would want to use my Bear Strategy explained elsewhere in this book and in my other books. If I am helping you manage your account you would know when to start using my Bear strategy for future buys and I would explain my logic to you.

You will see that my sell order was 3 contracts and I sold 4! That's because AIM is not a 100% computer-driven scientific investing method – it has some judgment calls. I felt Amazon was up so much in one month I wanted to sell 1 more contract because of such a large gain. When you get experienced with AIM every now and then you'll do the same thing!

Let's do the next month together. Try to predict ahead of time what to do.

TABLE 3

February 2018

Date Col. 1	Remarks Col. 2 AMZN 2020 S 1200	LEAPS Price Col. 3	LEAPS Value Col .4	Cash Col. 6	Contracts Bought (Sold) Col. 7	LEAPS Owned Col. 8	Portfolio Control Col. 9	Buy (Sell) Advice Col. 10	Market Order (Sell) Buy Col. 11	# Of Contracts Col. 13	Portfolio Value Col. 14
1/18		234.50	187600	145847	-`	800	156560	(31040)	(12280)	8	333,447
2/18		358.43	286744	146721	(4)	800	156560	(130184)	(143372)	8	433,465

Whenever you have a buy or sell trade it is necessary to recalculate your next minimum buy and sell orders. That is because your LEAPS Value and your CASH value have both changed. Updating the buy and sell prices after a trade are one of the most commonly asked requests for help I get from my clients and subscribers.

Let's go through the sale of four contracts in February as an example.

Below are my calculations for figuring your next AIM buy and sell after you sold 4 contracts in February 2018.

TABLE 4

Date Col. 1	Remarks Col. 2 AMZN 2020 S 1200	LEAPS Price Col. 3	LEAPS Value Col .4	Cash Col. 6	Contracts Bought (Sold) Col. 7	LEAPS Owned Col. 8	Portfolio Control Col. 9	Buy (Sell) Advice Col. 10	Market Order (Sell) Buy Col. 11	Portfolio Value Col. 12
Buy	3 Contracts	200.00	80000			400	156560	75560	68560	
Sell	2 Contracts	800.00	320000			400	156560	(163440)	(131440)	

Here's how I calculate the next buy and sell calculations.

What is your Portfolio Control? It is $156,560. This is the same as your original buy LEAPS Value.

Guess - what is the LEAPS value that would decrease enough to justify a Buy? From experience it will be at least 40% less. To start I tried $225.00, and then $200.00 and $200.00 worked to buy 3 contracts.

Portfolio Control $156,560 minus LEAPS Value $80,000 = $75,560 Buy Advice.

Next calculate the SAFE Value. It is 10% of your new LEAPS price so 10% of $80,000 is $8,000.

Subtract your SAFE Value from the Buy Advice. This lowers your Market Order to $68,560. You are left with $68,560 to buy more LEAPS.

The last step is to calculate how many contracts "fit" within this value. If 2 contracts is enough for a Buy then $68,560 divided by $20,000 (cost of one contract) = a buy of 3 contracts. So $68,560 gives you enough money to buy 3 contracts or 300 options. The actual math is $68,560 divided by $20,000 = buy 3.43 contracts but I rounded down to 3 contracts.

Two things to remember: you want a minimum of 15 contracts for each of your LEAPS so this a bad example for that insight. But it shows you what happens when you have too few contracts for AIM – you get a very high next Sell price. The new sell price is $800.00 an option or $80,000 a contract and you want a buy or sell price that let us buy or sell at least 2 contracts. I don't recommend just buying or selling one contract – you'll pay too much in commissions and lower your profits.

Here is the math for the Sell. I found from experience that the sell price will be about 40% higher than the original price or the current price after a previous buy or sell. So first I tried a sell price of $750 an option and found it wasn't high enough to let me sell two contracts. I keep it simple by using round numbers – so next I tried $800.00 and $800.00 let me sell 2 of my remaining 4 contracts. You see why I do calculations in pencil with a big eraser!

Here is the sell process one step at a time.

What is your Portfolio Control? It is $156,560. This is the same as your original buy Portfolio Control. The Portfolio Control did not change because you haven't had any buys yet.

What is the LEAPS value that would increase enough to justify a Sell? From experience it will be at least 40% more. To start I tried $750.00, and then $800.00 and $800.00 worked to sell 3 contracts. You'll see below we use $320,000 – not $800.00. That's because we need the total value of all 400 options (LEAPS) we own: $800.00 X 400 = $320,000.

Take the LEAPS Value $320,000 minus Portfolio Control $156,560 = $163,440. This is your Sell Advice.

Next calculate the SAFE Value. It is 10% of your new LEAPS price or 10% of $320,000 is $32,000.

Subtract your SAFE Value from the Sell Advice. This is $163,440 – SAFE $32,000 = $131,440. This is your Market Order.

The last step is to calculate how many contracts "fit" within this value. If 2 contracts are enough for a Sell then take $131,440 divided by $80,000 (the cost of one contract). So $131,440 gives you enough money to sell 2 contracts or 200 options. The actual math is $131,440 divided by $80,000 = sell 1.64 contracts so we round that up to 2 contracts. Here again you see the disadvantage of working with only a few contracts for particular LEAPS - your rounding has to be more aggressive or approximate.

In the above example, Robert Lichello and I would agree with the buy and sell prices because you could use the 10% SAFE amount to subtract from Buy (Sell) Advice. But when you are in a Bear Market you would run out of Cash too quickly before the LEAPS price hit bottom and started rising.

Then you would want to use my Bear Strategy explained elsewhere in this book. If I am helping you manage your account you would automatically start using my Bear strategy for future buys and explain my logic to you.

Now let's look at what actually happened in March with the AMZN example.

March 2018

Date Col. 1	Remarks Col. 2 AMZN 2020 S 1200	LEAPS Price Col. 3	LEAPS Value Col .4	Cash Col. 6	Contracts Bought (Sold) Col. 7	LEAPS Owned Col. 8	Portfolio Control Col. 9	Buy (Sell) Advice Col. 10	Market Order (Sell) Buy Col. 11	# Of Contracts Col. 13	Portfolio Value Col. 14
2/18		358.43	286744	146721	(4)`	800	156560	(130184)	(143372)	8	433,465
3/18	Ignore Sell	516.00	206400	291543	-	400	156560	(49840)	(29200)	4	497,943

There is no real difference updating your numbers EXCEPT for the important difference with Portfolio Control amount: **When you sell from your Portfolio, Portfolio Control stays the same. When you buy, Portfolio Control goes up by half the buy amount.**

Why you don't change Portfolio Control after a sell is because you have reduced the number of contracts you own so AIM works very well leaving Portfolio Control the same.

The 50-50 ratio between Cash and LEAPS Value will change up or down depending on a buy (cash goes down, LEAPS go up) or a sell (cash goes up, LEAPS go down). Most buys or sells barely move the 50-50 ratio to the point you should adjust this ratio.

A good rule of thumb is to wait for one of these amounts to be 100% higher than the other. So if LEAPS is $100,000 and Cash is $200,000 then add the two = $300,000 then divide by 2 and you see you should have $150,000 in LEAPS & $150,000 Cash. So you would buy another $50,000 worth of LEAPS. This happens when you have a great LEAPS that goes way up (you will have many) so sells are triggered. Adjusting Portfolio Control up 50% of the Buy amount has nothing to do with readjusting the LEAPS/Cash ratio.

Now when you buy more contracts, to keep AIM working correctly, you have to raise Portfolio Control by half of the Buy amount. That is how you do it in this situation. Once you use AIM you will see that raising Portfolio Control by half the buy amount will make you more profits because it will cause you to buy more contracts at a lower price and help you sell more contracts at a higher price.

Below you will see it is very easy to raise Portfolio Control by half your buy amount:

You buy $40,000 worth of LEAPS

Half that amount is $20,000

Portfolio Control was $300,000

You add half the buy amount ($20,000) and your new Portfolio Control is $320,000

Another famous AIM investor Tom Veale (who invented the Idiot Wave) also followed Lichello's guidance on this adjustment.

Robert Lichello invented AIM but didn't explain in his book why you need to increase Portfolio Control by 50%. I figured out like I explain above that raising Portfolio Control by 50% of buy amount will raise your long-term profits by giving you buys at a little higher price so you have more buys and delaying the number of contracts sold you can sell them at a higher price later. You are still getting excellent buys and sells now but making more profits later. You are NOT increasing your initial investment! You are only increasing Portfolio Control which is a "Control" number – NOT part of your investment!

One bonus insight about Limit Buys and Sells: if your buy is $200 the worst that can happen is you buy at $200 like you wanted. Even better is if the LEAPS is having a "Bear attack." You might buy those LEAPS at an even lower price like at $195 or $190! That happens because the price is moving so fast that the trade execution takes a few seconds and the prices continued to move in the direction that is good for you.

The same is true with sells – if your sell price is $450 worst that can happen is a sell at $450 but you may get a higher price than $450 like $455 or $460.

How to Set Up a Limit Trade Automatically with your Online Broker

Now that you know how to calculate the prices that justify a buy or sell, you are probably wondering how to set this up ahead of time with your broker so they happen automatically.

First, I want to emphasize how revolutionary and brilliant AIM has become for you. It has removed any need or worry to predict what the stock market will do! It is 100% reactive.

Why spend any time, money, or mental energy trying to predict what the stock market will do? The beauty of a contrarian investing strategy like AIM is that you can spend your time, money, and mental energy doing other things instead.

This is why <u>AIM investors have the most peace of mind of any active investor</u>. It doesn't matter whether the market goes up, goes down, or stays flat. Our investments will be making profits long-term no matter what! In the very worst case, our investments won't be losing money from the churning of trading commissions when it doesn't make any sense to trade in the first place. And our balance of 50% cash will be earning interest in the meantime!

Remember, this is investing for the long haul. I am teaching you a strategy that you can use for the rest of your life and your children's lives and your grandchildren's lives. Trying to predict ahead of time how and when various investments will change year after year requires that you never stop learning and watching the market, maybe on a daily basis. Why do that when you don't have to?

We don't have to guess whether the markets will go up or down. They always have - and they always will! Learn and master a method that profits from these ups and downs no matter when they happen and you will have gained a wealth-building system that will last the rest of your lifetime and through the lifetimes of your children and grandchildren.

Now I will show you how to set up these trades to happen automatically with an online broker. But I want to be sure you appreciate that I am showing you much more than how to do some simple mechanics on a website. If you are ready to harness the power of the "A" in AIM - Automatic Investment Management - here is how you can do it.

Note, I am going to show you how to do this with the TD Ameritrade website interface. As I said before, I don't have any financial ties to this company (other than all the commissions I have helped them earn through my trades and all the trades of people I have recommended them to over the years, which is a lot I'm sure.) But I have learned how to use their website, their commissions are lower than some other online brokers, and their customer service has been excellent for me whenever I call them. So here is how to place a limit buy or sell on TD Ameritrade. If you use a different online broker it will be similar.

First open your account and hover your cursor on **Trade**. In the pop-up window you will see **Options** in the second column. It should look like this:

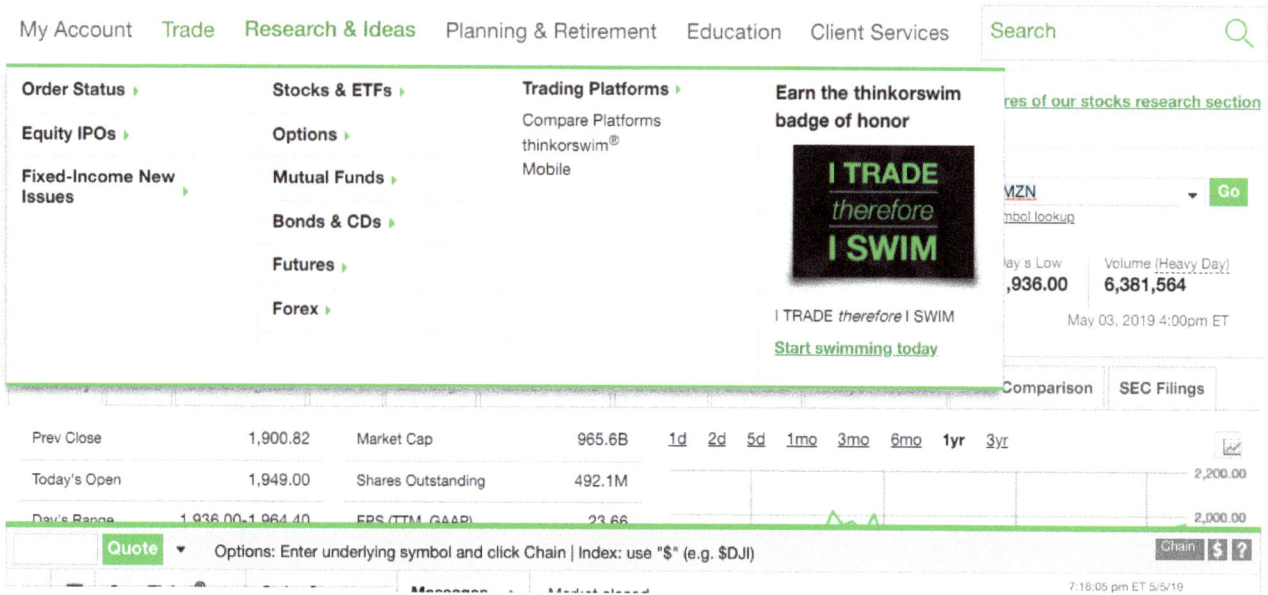

Click on **Options**: you will see this screen below. Values for this particular account have been masked. TD Ameritrade defaults to Options Strategy of Single order – you <u>always want single order</u> as your options strategy.

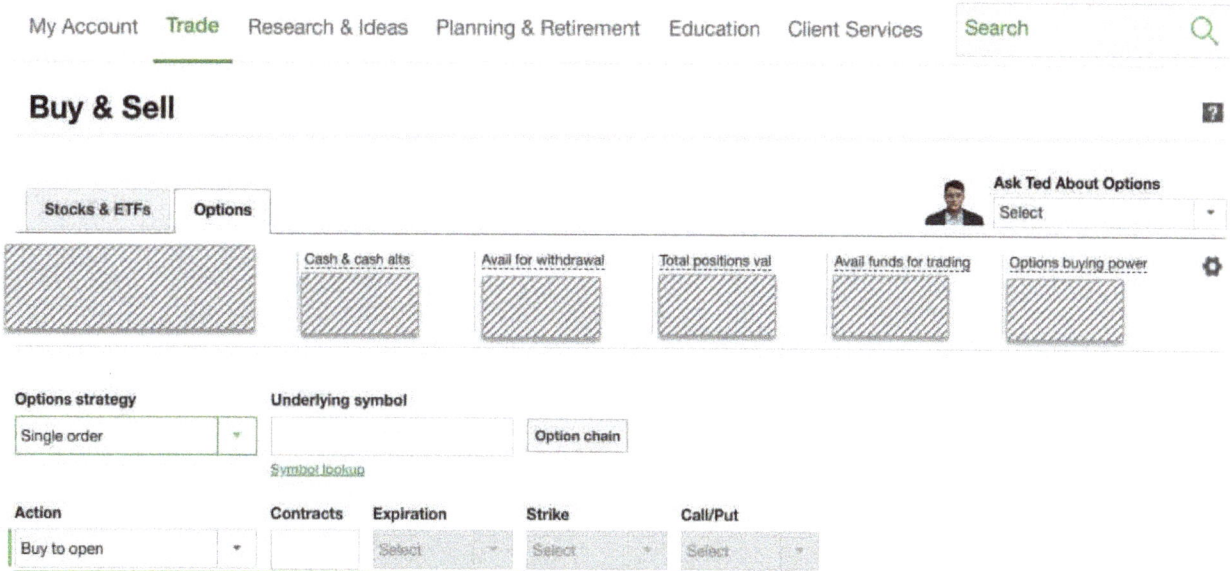

Next you enter the company ticker symbol you want in the "Underlying Symbol" box. For this example we will use Amazon which is AMZN. Type that in in the **Underlying symbol** box above. Then click the button next to it for **Option chain**. Then you should see something like this:

You need to look at the complete list of Options. Click the green **View full chain** link in the bottom right hand corner of the **Option chain** pop-up window. Then you'll see something like this:

You want to pick from the Options that are <u>farthest out into the future</u> that expire on the 3rd <u>Friday of the correct January</u>. Sometimes there are longer options on some LEAPS that expire in June. I don't want them because I don't like to roll over LEAPS in the middle of the year which is also the summer for me. We want to stick to January expiring 3rd Friday of January options (LEAPS).

In this case you'll see the LEAPS farthest out are January 2021. Whatever is at the bottom of the list, click the "+" sign and expand the group. This shows you all of the Strike Prices that are available as Calls and Puts. Since we currently own January 2021 LEAPS we will be rolling them over to January 2022 LEAPS in December 2019.

If you don't see the strike price you want or you want to be sure you see everything available, look at the top of the screen. The third filter option at the top row is called "**Range**."

Notice in this screenshot is says "**All**." Other choices are "In the Money," "Out of the Money," or "Near the Money." Click "All" like it is shown here and then you will see every strike price available. Remember after you change range to All with the down arrow you must refresh the page by clicking on the green **View Chain** at end of top row.

I normally recommend buying the Strike Price at or near the money (meaning the Strike Price is close to the stock price). When I manage and help an investor I go into detail about why I like a particular strike Price.

We will be buying Calls (we are bullish) about 99% of the time. Every so often I do see a stock that's in trouble and I would recommend using AIM with a Put but that's extremely rare.

After deciding the Strike Price you want for your Buy, click that hyperlink in the Call column. (ALMOST NEVER PUTS!) Calls are on the LEFT SIDE of the website. For this example I'm going to say Strike 1200. (That isn't actually shown in this screenshot. You would have to scroll down and then you would find it.)

Let's assume here that we are going to make a Buy. Click the small button just to the right of the "2100.0 Call" hyperlink that looks like a play button or a right facing arrow. When you do that it will open up a small pop-up window with more information and commands, including a link to Buy or Sell.

It will look like the next screenshot:

AMZN Sep 18 2020		497 Days to Expiration							
AMZN Jan 15 2021		616 Days to Expiration							Collapse
Calls	Bid	Ask	Last	High	Low	Change	Vol	Op Int	Strike
1870.0 Call	335.05	354.50	338.62	338.62	338.62	-16.99	1	13	1870.00
1880.0 Call	330.05	349.50	334.75	0.00	0.00	-15.77	2	88	1880.00
1890.0 Call	325.10	344.30	333.43	338.49	333.43	-11.99	5	73	1890.00
				332.38	321.00	-11.34	31	366	1900.00
				325.50	317.14	-9.74	2	37	1910.00
				312.23	312.23	-17.92	1	149	1920.00

AMZN Jan 15 2021 1890 Call

Buy | Sell | Add to watch list

| Bid | Ask | B/A Size | Volume | Open Interest |
| 325.10 | 344.30 | 2X2 | 5 | 73 |

| Last | Last Trade | | Net Change | % Change |
| 333.43 | 2019-05-09 12:44:15 EDT | | -11.99 | -3.47% |

| Open | Prev Close | High | Low | Time Value |
| 338.49 | 345.42 | 338.49 | 333.43 | 323.56 |

Real time quote provided by OPRA @ 1:47:57 AM EDT

Add to watch list

...tions trading may expose investors to potentially rapid and substantial losses. Please read ...ions.

Before investing in a mutual fund or ETF, be sure to carefully consider the fund's or ETF's investing objectives, risks, charges and expenses. For a prospectus containing this and other important information, contact the fund or ETF sponsor, or a TD Ameritrade Client Services representative. Please read the prospectus carefully before investing.

Client Agreement | Privacy Statement | Security Center | Privacy Monitor

Click the type of trade you want, which in this case is a Buy. Then you'll get a screen that looks like this:

Notice that your LEAPS is now reflected in the Options field (the Company, expiration date, Strike Price, and Call order). Your Order Type is also **Limit** which is what you want. Limit order means the trade will only happen if and when the price is met.

Also important - the **Time-in-force** at the end of row – make sure it always says **GTC** or **Good-til-Canceled**. Your broker keeps a GTC open usually for 3 months – that's what the Date box below GTC means. Your broker will automatically fill any limit order buy or sell order when it either hits the buy price or sell price.

There are many other settings here to understand and choose.

Action will always be either Buy to Open or Sell to Close. **NEVER BUY TO CLOSE or SELL TO OPEN!**

Routing is Smart. Smart routing means your stock broker offers your buy or sell to several order-makers. They will fill it at the lowest buy price or highest sell price.

Those selections should be used every time. Next you have to enter the number of Contracts to Buy or Sell and your Limit Price. Let's say it is 3 Contracts for this example and a Limit option Buy of $200.00. That means $20,000 a contract (100 options at $200.00 each). Remember options are priced by option not by contract (which is 100 options).

Also remember to look at the expiration of your GTC limit orders. You will not get a notification when they are about to expire. I recommend you create a calendar reminder to keep track of these expirations ahead in 3 months.

This is everything you need. Double-check everything and when you like it click the **Review Order** button on the right of the window. You will get a new screen like this:

If everything looks good, you click the **Place Order** button. Note that you have 90 seconds to do it or the order will time out on TD Ameritrade – your broker may be different.

Congratulations, you've set your future AIM trade!

You will repeat this for every LEAPS, creating both a limit buy and limit sell order. Then your automatic trades will be ready to go whether your LEAPS go up or down.

Two very important things to remember: **IT IS ALWAYS <u>BUY TO OPEN</u> AND <u>SELL TO CLOSE</u>!** *NEVER "BUY to CLOSE" OR "SELL TO OPEN!!!!"*

"Buy to open" is a term used by brokerages to represent the establishment of a new (opening) long call or put position in options. A **buy to open** order indicates to market participants that the trader is establishing a new position rather than closing out an existing position.

Sell to close is an options trading order that is used to exit a trade in which the trader already owns the options contract and must **sell** the contract to **close** the position.

You "buy" options (LEAPS) when you "open" a position. You now own say 15 contracts – then you set up your spreadsheet to actively use AIM to buy and sell contracts. You only own LEAPS' contracts if you "BUY to OPEN."

Buy to close is the purchase of an option position. A trader will **buy** an asset to offset, or **close**, a short position in that same asset. Essentially, it is the **buying** back of an asset initially sold short. **You will NEVER Buy to Close!**

You are NOT buying back a position you originally sold short! There is also a big risk difference between Buying to Open & Buying to Close. When you buy to open your risk is limited to the amount of the LEAPS you bought. So if you buy $5,000 worth of LEAPS the most you lose is $5,000.

But with Buy to Close you are subject to potentially unlimited losses if the trade goes against you. **Don't worry about understanding Buy to Close – just remember to NEVER DO IT! - Always "Buy to Open"!**

Sell to open refers to instances in which an option investor initiates, or opens, an option trade by **selling** or establishing a short position in an option. This enables the option seller to receive the premium paid by the buyer on the opposite side of the transaction. A good example is selling Covered Calls on stocks you own.

You are **NEVER** opening a short position – you don't need to understand this because you will NEVER "SELL to OPEN" - it's always "**Sell to Close**." When your LEAPS that you own from Buying to Open go up higher enough to generate a sell AIM wants you to sell some contracts and turn paper profits into real profits. Again you could suffer large losses from Sell to Open – Again you will NEVER use Sell to Open!

You are always "long" with AIM. With calls being long means you want the stock and the LEAPS to go higher - you are Bullish. Sophisticated investors who at least think they know what they are doing can "short" either stocks or options. Let's leave that strategy to them – we want to have a "keep it simple" options strategy.

> *With AIM my action is already determined for me. Makes for*
> *stress free investing. Taking profits! System is great.*
>
> **- Hunter B., JJJ Investing Services subscriber**

For all of your LEAPS you want to set up these Limit orders for both the buys and sells. This means that whether the market goes up or down your AIM buys and sells will be automatically set to trade.

If the prices never reach those limit buy or sell prices, AIM tells you that your most profitable action is to do nothing. Why pay commissions to brokers so they make profits instead of you? You only want to trade when you are guaranteed to be investing into a bargain or selling to convert your paper profits into real profits.

Now you should have all the information you need to turn your investing into an

AUTOMATED process. For those people who prefer to get my help calculating the new buy and sell limit prices after every trade that is one of the many things I do for my clients. If you would like to get my help for a few months to make your learning faster and have my help to check your work, I invite you to contact me through my website or my contact information listed in the end of the book.

At this point, some people still think that AIM is too good to be true or it must have some fundamental flaws, otherwise more people would know about it and be using it. Or maybe it worked before but there's no guarantee it will work in the future. Why aren't professional investing advisors recommending AIM to their clients?

These are fair questions and concerns. I'll be glad to answer them all for you.

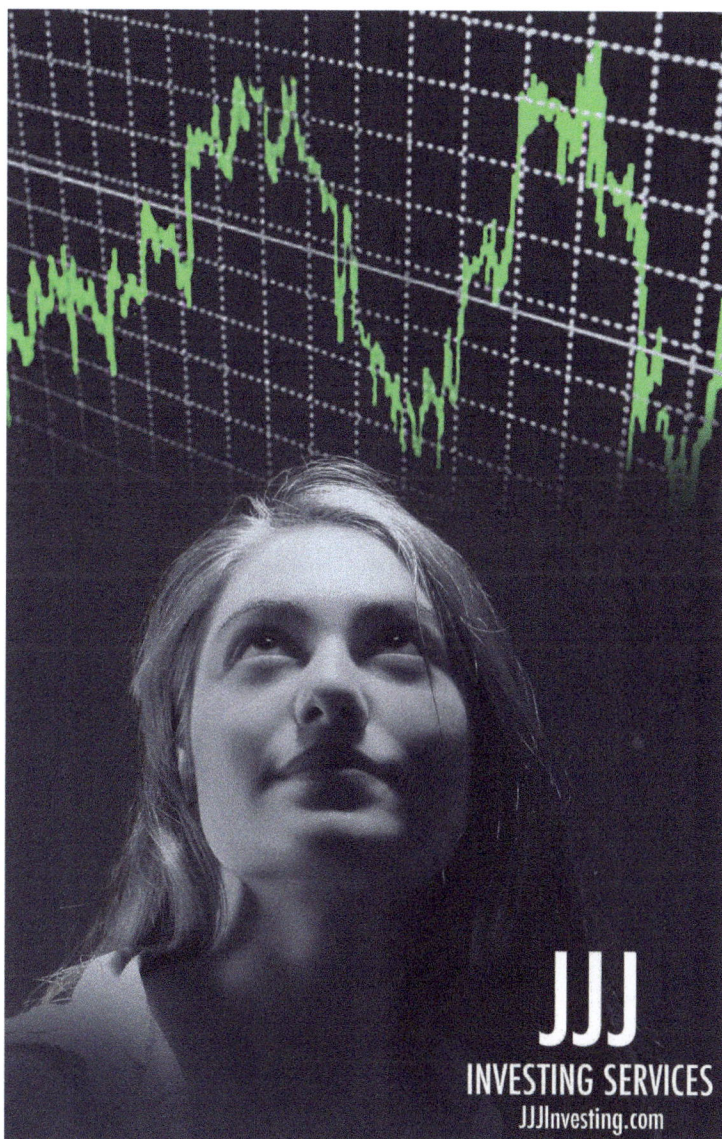

CHAPTER 8

Major Objections to AIM With LEAPS (And My Responses)

In the spring of 2018, my business partner Brett and I released a survey to ask people why they aren't using the AIM investing method yet. This survey went to all of my newsletter subscribers and blog post subscribers. I also shared this survey to all my followers on social media - Facebook, LinkedIn, and Twitter. (I have almost 160,000 followers on Twitter - mostly investing fans and investors - so it had a respectable reach.)

In the survey we also identified people who actually had started using AIM. To them we asked: what is their biggest challenge with AIM – Automatic Investment Management?

We appreciate everyone who replied.

The responses fell into a few major categories. We saw these as a list of objections, misconceptions, or lack of understanding about the AIM method. Here they are along with my responses.

If you were hoping to find answers to a specific question or concern about the AIM method when you bought this book, I hope you find it in the list below.

Challenge #1: Lack of knowledge about AIM

A lot of people said they aren't using AIM for reasons like these:

"Lack of know-how."

"Would like direct coaching to make sure I understand it correctly."

"I want guidance on AIM."

"Need guidance on investing."

"Getting started with AIM."

"Planning how to use AIM."

"Would like direct coaching to make sure I understand AIM correctly."

My answer:

Hopefully you are now much better off than these people because you have this book in front of you!

If you still feel like you want to learn more about AIM, here are 5 specific things you can do:

1. Read the many blog articles on my website (all FREE): www.jjjinvesting.com

2. Sign up for free to receive future blog articles: http://www.jjjinvesting.com/free-sign-ups

3. Follow me on social media. The one I recommend most is @jjjinvesting on Twitter.

4. Request a COMPLIMENTARY "FREE LOOK" SUBSCRIPTION to my monthly newsletter: http://www.jjjinvesting.com/free-sign-ups

5. Request a FREE PDF of my first book about AIM. It's over 350 pages if you print it on 8.5x11 paper (which I recommend). It is called "I Guarantee You Will Buy Low, Sell High, and Make Money." Request that on the same page here: http://www.jjjinvesting.com/free-sign-ups

If you are the kind of person that is used to personal attention and professional service, you can have my personal help for 6 months or longer. I will educate you on the best AIM LEAPS investments based on the amount of money you have to invest and what your investing goals are.

I will also set up your original spreadsheets and show you your next buy and sell prices on updated spreadsheets.

I will look up your LEAPS closing prices and advise you on whether you have a buy, sell or do nothing every day the stock market is open.

I can call you on a regular basis and let you know how your investments are doing. You are very welcome to ask me any questions you have and learn AIM and grow your knowledge every time we talk.

After 6 months of my daily help you will be very knowledgeable about all aspects of using my AIM investing method.

You can decide to continue having me help you on a regular basis or can do AIM on your own at that point. If you want to become self-reliant with AIM, I will be happy to get you there.

We may only talk when I see that you are near a buy or sell. Some clients prefer it that way. You don't need to check your AIM portfolio every day. As you should have learned in the earlier chapter, when you set your next buy and sell prices as "Good Till Canceled" or GTC, the AIM system automatically does your buying and selling for you. Then you tell me your buy or sell information (what price and how many contracts were traded, and then I update your spreadsheets with the next buy and sell).

That's the beauty of AIM!

If you want to know how to get my help for the next 6 months, please contact me through my website www.jjjinvesting.com or email me at jeff@jjjinvesting.biz. My rates have been increasing in recent years due to increased demand so I am not putting them here in the book. Please go to my website to find my current rates.

Challenge #2: I'm afraid I will lose money in the market

My response:

You need to be more concerned with <u>not making profits</u> from the stock market. The AIM investing method is very safe for several reasons:

- Half your portfolio is always kept in cash.

- Your trades are based on pre-calculated price changes that only make sense because they will generate profits for you.

- You are never at risk of holding options when they expire.

This strategy has worked for over 25 years and will continue to work as long as the market has ups and downs. You will have "paper" losses at times but you use those dips to buy more LEAPS contracts at bargain prices.

They will go up later and make you real profits.

You might be wondering, what if those prices never go up again? That's where picking the right stocks for AIM is important. My Dogs of the Dow portfolio is one of my favorites. It has stocks that will last a long time. The Dogs of the Dow are the 10 stocks that pay the highest dividends. These are companies like Verizon, IBM, Exxon Mobile, Proctor and Gamble, GE, and Coca-Cola.

You might have temporary paper losses when the LEAPS from these companies go down. But do you really think the prices will be permanently down? No, these companies will be around for a long time. (And if it looks like they won't be, we adjust quickly.)

The reason most people don't succeed in the stock market is because they let their emotions get the better of them. It's either greed or fear. Or both. AIM solves that because it is a scientific and systematic way to always buy low, sell high, or do nothing.

If you are afraid of losing money you should be more afraid of being a victim to your fear for the rest of your life. You are missing out on the great benefits of AIM which eliminates the worry and uncertainty about what happens with the market. AIM will make buy and sell decisions for you!

Challenge #3: I'm an international investor (not in the United States)

Some people think that trading U.S. companies isn't allowed when they live overseas. One person said trading fees in Singapore were excessive.

My answer:

I have an investor in Australia and another in Japan who can trade American stocks and LEAPS.

Ask around or look online and you will likely be able to find a stock broker in your country who lets you trade American investments.

One person said trading commissions are high in Singapore. AIM will make you very high profits that will offset high commissions. Check with your friends in Singapore who invest and see if there is a cheaper way to invest that what you are currently doing.

Situation #4: I like other investing methods better

Some people gave responses like these:

"I fully understand the technical mechanism of AIM's position-sizing dynamics and for myself there are more attractive active-management strategies available."

"Comparing it with value averaging I like that better."

"I've been preoccupied doing other investment techniques."

My response:

If you have a better way of investing then you should stick with it. Please compare to AIM which, in one example, $60,000 ($30,000 LEAPS with Dogs of the Dow and $30,000 Cash) has grown 539% in 5 years and 6 months. My Dow Jones portfolio of 10 DJIA stocks (not the LEAPS) has increased 1,013% from September 1993 to June 2019 when I write this.

When you read my newsletter you will routinely see growth of 20-30% per year in various portfolios.

AIM has what every investment method should have: the contrarian approach to buying low and selling high. The basic AIM strategy will help you in other areas of investing like cryptocurrencies if you are trading those. I recommend you check the actual profits your current investing method. Be scientific and analytical about it, not emotional. Compare those profits to the profits you would make with AIM.

Challenge #5: Lack of motivation

We received responses like these:

"It's probably laziness on my part."

"I have not checked it out enough yet."

My response:

It is refreshing to see this honesty and self-awareness. There is an easy solution: hire me to do the work for you. I will help you manage your portfolio. I won't be lazy. You can still be lazy and will be able to benefit from AIM as I do the work for you.

Challenge #6: Not enough money to invest with AIM

People told us things like these

"I'm low on cash"

"lack of funds"

"Nothing to invest"

"not enough funding"

"Money shortage"

"not enough funds to start"

My response:

Many people are surprised to learn that you can start investing with AIM using as little as $1,000. The challenge here is to find LEAPS that are low enough price to allow for a portfolio of companies with this small amount. There aren't many to choose from but it is possible.

For those who want to invest in FAANGs, you will need a large sum of money. I conservatively recommend starting with at least $500,000. I've added a FAANGS portfolio with 10 FAANGs and FAANG-Like LEAPS that will start with about $20,000,000. You don't need to start with that large amount – I can help you find 3-5 good FAANGs or FAANG-like LEAPS spending around $1,000,000 – 2,000,000 per FAANG. You will be able to own enough contracts (at least 15-20) to easily trade using AIM and make fantastic long-term profits.

Here is how you can start without any money: you can learn AIM by using a paper trading account. Pick the stocks or LEAPS that you think will be a good investment. Then do your calculations for a limit buy and sell. Watch the price and wait for it to reach one of those prices. When it does, update your spreadsheet as if the trade happened. Then continue to do this paper trading until you feel comfortable with the process.

You will quickly learn to invest using AIM. Then when you do have money we can set up a real AIM trading account.

Challenge #7: Lack of time to test & validate AIM

Some people said they want to "back test" AIM, which means looking backward in time to see how AIM would have done now that you know how prices went up and down over time.

My answer:

You don't need to back test it because I have already done that - with many portfolios (each with many companies) over many decades. Look at my newsletter and you will see one portfolio of the same 10 stocks using AIM since 1993 – 26 years ago. That portfolio is up 1,013% as of June 2019.

Another LEAPS portfolio is 13 years old as of 2019. It through the financial meltdown of 2008-2009. The "In the Money LEAPS" portfolio is up 765% as of June 2019.

Perhaps what these people really need is a better understanding of how AIM works. Once you understand it you will know that back testing is an academic exercise. As long as prices go up or down AIM makes the trading decisions for you. It works every time because it is a robust strategy.

People learn by different methods. Some have to read, some people watch, some like to listen, and some learn by doing. Think about how you learn best and then contact me so we can do it together. I have some videos on YouTube if you search for JJJ Investing there. Or we can set a time for me to explain it to you over the phone or a video call. That is how most people learn it best, we've found.

Concern #8: Shouldn't I have heard about AIM (or AIM with LEAPS) from mainstream investing news sources or my financial advisor?

My response:

Robert Lichello developed AIM in the 1970s. I have heard that he sold more than a million books and wrote several updates. I still hear from many people that have heard of AIM. They aren't exactly sure what it is but know it was very successful in its day.

One simple and sad reason we don't hear about AIM much now is that Lichello passed away in 2001 at the age of 74. He was a lone voice on a mission to spread the word about AIM and didn't name anyone else to continue his work on his behalf after he was gone. Even legendary AIM investor Tom Veale, creator of The Idiot Wave, never used LEAPS with AIM. He did tell me in a Facebook post he thought AIM with LEAPS was a great idea!

Another good reason you haven't heard of AIM lately is that it really doesn't work well with almost all stocks. Stocks cost too much for the average investor and they just are not volatile enough to really be effective with AIM. I have a friend Greg who is a financial advisor. He told me he learned about AIM many years ago and discarded it because it didn't work well with stocks. Then he came to one of presentations and told me I was brilliant for combining AIM with long-term options (LEAPS).

I have been told by a former licensed investing advisor that my AIM investing method with LEAPS is very effective, is safe, and works very well. But he told me he could never recommend my AIM investing method to his clients because financial advisors are not allowed to recommend any investments that earn higher than 12% a year. You can see from the results documented in this book that AIM with LEAPS can't be recommended because it performs too well!

He told me he thinks this is because the licensing requirements are designed to protect the big boys like mutual funds, annuities, banks, etc. They don't want competition from an effective and safe way to invest. So virtually no financial advisor could even recommend this way of investing to clients even if they wanted to.

Also, the Securities & Exchange Commission (SEC) thinks ordinary investors are too dumb to understand options. Investors have to read a booklet from SEC on understanding the risks of options and have to apply separately to their broker to get permission to trade options.

Generally, stock brokers aren't going to recommend any option investments unless the investor insists. And one very prominent Stock Broker (a name you would recognize) will not let their independent advisors sell options (including covered calls) to their clients!

Finally, AIM with LEAPS is not a passive investing strategy. 99.99% of investors (and therefore the news and people marketing to them) make an investment and then only look at their quarterly statements (if that) or wait until an annual review with their advisor to make any adjustments. You don't see many mainstream sources or financial advisors catering to active traders. But if you want to earn more profits than 99.99% of all investors over the long haul; an active yet safe, easy, quick, and scientific method like AIM with LEAPS is exactly what you need.

So I am the voice crying in the Wilderness. I am the guy carrying the candle in the dark to educate investors on this safe, reliable, long-term investing method that will give them remarkable profits in a world that gets tougher every day financially. Hardly anyone gets pensions anymore. Companies seem to be shifting to short term benefits like health club memberships instead of contributing to employee 401k's.

Then there is the fact that more and more people aren't staying with companies long enough to get vested in any retirement benefits. More and more people are freelancing and being entrepreneurial.

Standard investments like mutual funds, CDs, and annuities will never grow your money enough for a great retirement. Sharing AIM + LEAPS is my mission to help you have the great future you want and deserve.

You can't blame me for keeping AIM + LEAPS a secret! I have written three books on AIM and published a monthly newsletter for over 26 years. I have been marketing my AIM method on Twitter, Facebook, LinkedIn, and even YouTube. I have marketed AIM to my friends and at Meet-up events.

Every week new people sign up to get my blog posts and my newsletter. However you learned about AIM, just be glad you did. These are many reasons why you won't learn about it from large institutional and traditional sources. That's another sign that you have found a legitimate contrarian investing method - which AIM + LEAPS certainly is!

CHAPTER 9
Special Cases With AIM Investing

After you have been using the AIM method for a few months (or years - or decades in my case) you will run into situations that make you wonder what to do. Here are some of those special situations:

- How to earn higher yields or interest on your AIM Cash

- How to roll over LEAPS from one year to the next

- How to adjust your strategy in a severe BEAR market

- How to re-adjust your Cash / LEAPS ratio when it gets out of whack

- How to add more money into your portfolio

- What happens if you skip or miss a month

In this chapter I will give you an executive-level summary for most of these topics. I have written extensively about all of them in my other books including my first book which I now offer for free as a PDF if you ask me for it. Some of these cases I have addressed in this book already.

Here I will do my best to condense the main points so you can see that there is a way to address all of these contingencies. The details and nuances can take many more pages or conversations but this should assure you that there is a safe and systematic way to handle all of them.

How to Earn Higher Yields or Interest on your AIM Cash

This book is geared for wealthier investors. So it's possible someone might start with $1,000,000 in LEAPS and $1,000,000 in CASH. You don't want that cash money idly sitting in the Broker's Money Market Account earning practically zero interest!

Here is my safe way to increase your profits and still always have plenty of cash to buy when AIM says Buy.

Take half your cash (also 1/4th your total portfolio) and buy high yielding Real Estate Investment Trusts (REITS) and/or high-yield income Closed-End Funds.

By law, REITS have to pay out 90% of their profits to shareholders. This makes them much better than CDs (Certificates of Deposit) which pay a pitiful 1-2% (as I write this in 2019). As you will see below, REITS pay very high yields. Many of them pay monthly dividends!

As a rule of thumb I recommend you put half your AIM cash into REITS. You can always sell some shares of the REIT if you need more cash to buy LEAPS! So look below and check some of these out.

If you have $1,000,000 cash for AIM, invest $500,000 in REITS and you average roughly 1% return monthly. If you have $500,000 in REITS it will pay you $5,000 a month or better. That may not seem like a lot compared to your $1M in cash but think about the peace of mind and security you have with all that cash (protecting you from a stock market crash) plus you are still earning more than most Americans earn every month just on the yield - let's be grateful.)

This is just one more way I will help you make the highest possible profits! While being a safe and savvy investor!

The prices listed in the following table are as of December 5, 2018.

SYMBOL	52-WEEK HIGH	52 WEEK LOW	% YIELD	PAYS DIVIDEND	CURRENT PRICE
AGNC	$20.84	$17.26	12.2%	MONTHLY	$17.64
NLY	$12.37	$9.70	9.7%	MONTHLY	$10.03
AWP	$6.98	$5.34	10.97%	MONTHLY	$5.47
CHCT	$32.81	$22.41	5.3%	QUARTERLY	$30.28
OHI	$38.34	$24.90	6.98%	QUARTERLY	$37.94
STWD	$23.04	$19.47	8.6%	QUARTERLY	$22.32
LTC	$47.99	$34.46	5%	MONTHLY	$45.63
ARI	$19.57	$17.56	9.71%	QUARTERLY	$18.95
WPG	$8.44	$5.40	16.72%	QUARTERLY	$5.98
AHOTF	$7.62	$4.92	12.93%	MONTHLY	$5.01
UNIT	$23.42	$13.94	12.41%	QUARTERLY	$19.34
TRSWF	$10.71	$7.64	8.43%	MONTHLY	$8.45
PSEC	$7.60	$5.95	10.56%	MONTHLY	$6.82
LAND	$13.95	$11.36	4.05%	MONTHLY	$13.17
LXP	$10.61	$7.69	8.36%	QUARTERLY	$8.49
APLE	$20.19	$15.56	7.66%	MONTHLY	$15.66
CJREF	$9.47	$2.75	5.03%	MONTHLY	$3.61
TCO	$66.61	$49.64	5.13%	QUARTERLY	$51.11
EPR	$72.18	$51.87	6.2%	MONTHLY	$69.66
CBL	$6.26	$2.39	12.5%	QUARTERLY	$2.40

Two REITS currently (in June 2019) are paying over 10% a year dividends. And they pay them monthly! Those two are AGNC & NLY.

I don't know about you, but I am happy to know some people that treat me to a nice steak dinner every time they see me because of just this bit of advice that has transformed the returns on their substantial cash savings.

Rolling over LEAPS to Next Year's LEAPS

Many times with AIM you will want to continue investing with the company for many years. But since LEAPS expire after two years what is the best way to continue to own LEAPS on the same stock? It's easy: you just sell the prior LEAPS and roll over the Portfolio Total amount into next year's LEAPS.

Next year's LEAPS come out every September, October, and November. So by December all of next year's LEAPS are ready to be bought.

In previous books, I have shown spreadsheets for the specific details. When you are a client of mine I do this for you. Here is this process at a high level:

1. Recognize when the next year's LEAPS have been released.

2. Sell or liquidate all of your LEAPS on this stock for your current holding.

3. Look at your new Portfolio Value for this company (LEAPS Value + Cash).

4. Invest half of this amount into the next year's LEAPS.

With this process you have actually done two good things:

1. You have extended your options by another year.

2. You have re-balanced your portfolio on this LEAPS to be 50% LEAPS and 50% cash.

One thing I didn't mention: you need to decide what Strike Price your new LEAPS will be at.

How do decide what Strike Price to buy with your cash? We rarely will be buying the same Strike Price from one year to the next. The underlying stock probably went up or down during the year. In this case, a better Strike Price is one close to what the stock is selling at in the month you make this rollover.

The other factor you need to consider is that you always want at least 10 contracts of your

LEAPS. If there is any question, pick the higher Strike Price so that you have at least this many contracts.

Weighing all the factors that go into picking the Strike Price are worth a chapter in itself. I wrote about this in my first book that is over 300 pages long which you can get for free if you ask me. I explain the factors to my clients when I help them decide what strike price is best for their particular goals, risk tolerances, and outlooks for the particular LEAPS.

During this end-of-the-year rollover you may also decide that it is time to divest completely from a company and then pick a different company for the next year.

How to Use LEAPS in a Severe BEAR Market

It's near the end of January 2019 as I write this. The stock market has had a pretty severe bear market for the past half a year or more. And this bear market has severely affected our model LEAPS portfolio. I have found that LEAPS react quite severely in a BEAR market. Also LEAPS react quite strongly when a stock becomes a BEAR that isn't going to recover (remember Enron?).

Based on actual real world experience, I am writing this section to see what we can do about severe BEAR markets that will improve the performance of our LEAPS. Also what can we do to prevent ourselves from being stuck with the investment that offers little or no hope of a recovery?

Two painful lessons taught me about this strategy. The first was with Advanced Micro Devices (AMD). I thought it was a good company for the long haul but the stock price kept going down for many years. This was before I was using LEAPS.

The same thing happened with Crocs, a unique type of Shoe Company that went all the way down from $22 to $1 and then went back up into the $30s. CROC is an example of a stock that performed exactly like LEAPS. You can see 5 years of CROC up and down history in the last chapter of my full-length original book.

In reviewing how I handled AMD, I find I wasn't aggressive enough in waiting to buy when the price of the LEAPS went down. I just wasn't aware that LEAPS could sink so far in a BEAR market. In the future when you own a LEAPS, you must really analyze when to buy and how much to buy in a BEAR Market. In the future I will take a much stronger stance and will wait to buy initially in the down market at about 30% lower than the original purchase price. Then starting with the 2nd buy I'd go to my Bear Strategy.

A good rule of thumb would be to start using Bear Strategy on your 2nd buy. This is a sign that you are in Bear territory. Use a buy price 50% less than your first buy price. **Let the LEAPS drop 50% before making your 2nd buy in a BEAR Market.** So for example if your 2nd buy of LEAPS was $4 a share or $400 a contract then you wait until the LEAPS drops to $2.00 or $200 a contract and then you make your first BEAR buy.

Here is a second Bear Strategy rule: only buy the number of contracts you can buy with 1/3 of your remaining cash.

For example you have $30,000 cash remaining and your next buy is at $2000. Regular AIM (10% SAFE) might give you a buy of 8 contracts for $16,000. But that will wipe out a lot of your Cash – so you follow my rule and only use 1/3 of your remaining cash to buy 5 contracts ($10,000). Then the next buy automatically is 50% less or $100.00 an option or $1,000 a contract and you would buy 7 contracts for $7,000. I try to keep the bear strategy simple and always automatically apply it when I help people manage their account. When I call friends I teach them this bear strategy so someday they can fully use AIM by themselves.

If I had used the strategy of waiting until the price dropped 50% with AMD, I would not have bought more shares too soon. Making several buys in succession was a clue that I was in extreme BEAR territory and should have adjusted my strategy.

Then if you check the last 10 years of AMD you'll see the stock had a remarkable run from 2008 – 2019.

Based on my experiences with AMD and other non-Dow Jones LEAPS I decided that you should limit yourself to "blue chips" LEAPS like the FAANGS (conservative ones but expensive and limited to rich investors to use with AIM) initially. Or you really need to understand how volatile a non-blue-chip could be before you purchase it as an initial

LEAPS in your portfolio and be able to handle the emotional and financial risks. Even if you buy a conservative LEAPS, that doesn't mean you will eliminate the risk entirely. The nature of the beast is that LEAPS will always be a lot more volatile than the stock it derives its value from. Even on very conservative stocks, LEAPS can fall sharply.

Remember my cardinal rule for initial investing: **buy at or near the 52-week low.** But even with that strategy, you can't guarantee that you will buy at the absolute bottom. So even with the "conservative" FAANG LEAPS, you run the chance of a sharp drop before the LEAPS recover. Again be cautious on when to make the buys and be cautious on how much you buy. AIM should always be one part of your total investment strategy and portfolio.

Re-adjusting the Cash / LEAPS Ratio

At least once a year, you should re-adjust the LEAPS/cash ratio to whatever ratio you are using for your particular type of investment. Usually this is 50/50. During the course of a year with buys and sells this can become unbalanced.

The best time for this is when the LEAPS make a big drop. For example, ALIBABA went from $43.65 to $18.40 in one month. After adjusting for this change in the model portfolio (found in my newsletter), we went from owning 268 contracts to 459 contracts.

My standard advice is to do this re-adjustment when you roll over all of your LEAPS from one year to the next. You will be selling all of your older LEAPS anyway. Doing this full adjustment and re-balancing is one of the services I provide for my clients so I do encourage you to take advantage of my expertise and service in this regard.

If the CASH balance is higher than 1/2 of the LEAPS VALUE I take the excess CASH and buy more LEAPS. If the CASH balance is less than ½ of the LEAPS VALUE, you want to sell enough of your LEAPS to get closer to the 50/50 ratio.

Adding Additional Money

There could be situations when you see how well AIM is working that you want to add more money into your investment account.

Adding money into your portfolio is good to do for three reasons:

1. It increases the size of your investment (including your cash reserve).

2. It decreases the relative cost of commissions.

3. Best of all - it increases your profits!

There are two other important factors to factor into your decision:

1. If you don't have at least 10 companies in your portfolio to diversify and spread the risk (always a good rule), use your additional money to increase your diversification.

2. If you are adding money into existing companies, only do this when your price is at or near its 52-week low.

If all of these conditions are true this could be a good time to add cash into your AIM portfolio.

Skipping A Month

Yet another benefit of AIM is that it is forgiving if you don't check it every month. (Compare this to the chore and stranglehold of those who are day-trading and can't even afford to be away for a single day!)

This is possible because you set your buys and sells ahead of time based on the formulas. They will happen without you checking on them. Your only task each month is to update the new buy and sell trades based on whatever trades happened while you were living and enjoying the rest of your life while AIM continued to work automatically with big profits for you. Again this is how Mr. Spock would invest, not Dr. Bones McCoy!

If you haven't received a notice of a buy or sell in a given month from your brokerage account or from me, it means you didn't have any buys or sells in your AIM portfolio. In that case it is fine to do nothing for that month because that is what AIM is telling you. But if you did have any buys or sells you do want to recalculate your new buy and sell price for those LEAPS.

The chance is low that you will hit your updated buy or sell price on a LEAPS soon after a trade in one month as you might guess. Still, if it does happen you want to be prepared and ready with the next buy and sell prices ready to trade automatically. That is another benefit of working with me to watch your AIM portfolio for you - I will quickly calculate your updated buy and sell prices, send you a new spreadsheet, and let you know when you are getting close to a buy or sell price for any of your LEAPS or stocks.

CHAPTER 10 (BONUS)

Sample Newsletter from JJJ Investing Services

When you are one of my clients, in addition to all of the personal attention and service you receive, you will also get my monthly investing newsletter. As of April 2019, I have been writing and publishing this newsletter for more than 26 years. It gets delivered to your email a day or two before the month begins.

Some subscribers read it right away on their phone or computer. Others like to download the PDF version that is available through a link, print it out on old-fashioned paper, and read it on the train when they go to work or at the kitchen table with their coffee in the morning.

As a preview for you and thanks for buying this book, I am including the May 2019 newsletter for you to see. If you like the idea of getting this newsletter for free for a limited time, stay tuned for instructions to do that.

First, let me make a few comments about this particular May 2019 issue:

- I am continuously looking and listening for ways to improve my newsletter (along with everything I do for my clients). If there are any changes, I highlight those at the beginning of the newsletter. This was the second month that I streamlined the number of portfolios in order to focus on those most valuable portfolios, eliminate some redundancy, and frankly make my job easier each month so I can focus more time on serving my growing list of clients.

- You will see a mention about my next book coming out. You are reading that result right now! I have removed that section from the newsletter because you obviously don't need to read that at this point.

- Both the email and the PDF version include hyperlinks to websites, books, and other resources that are mentioned. Most of those links have been removed here.

- The newsletter doesn't have a Table of Contents but long-time subscribers know that it follows a consistent format every month. Here is what you will see:

- Header, Specials in this Issue, Welcome, Dedication

- Monthly investing Anecdote

- AIM Tip of the Month

- Book Review of the month

- Website Recommendation of the month

- Newsletter Publication Information

- AIM Reference Website

- Disclaimers

- AIM Good Buy (Good Start) Recommendations

- Investment Portfolio Updates

  - Dogs of the Dow LEAPS (started January 2014)

  - DJIA Stocks (started September 1993!)

  - Dogs of the Dow STOCKS (started January 2014)

  - In the Money LEAPS (started August 2006)

  - FAANG + CHINA LEAPS (started January 2016)

  - DJIA Out of the Money LEAPS (started September 2016)

  - FAANG High Value LEAPS (started April 2019)

Vol. 26 No. 5 – May 2019

THE JJJ INVESTING NEWSLETTER
BUY LOW - SELL HIGH - MAKE MONEY

Copyright 2019 by
JJJ Investing Services

From Jeff Weber, Author of
HERE ARE THE CUSTOMERS' YACHTS

Special in this Issue: Jeff's next book is underway - and you can be a part of it!

Welcome to the 26th year of this newsletter! Look and you will see the Dow Jones Industrial Average (those boring stocks) have grown from $15,000 to over $163,200. The Dow portfolio is up 988% since September 1993, over 26 years later. And friends have turned me on to an even better way to play the Dow – using the Dogs of the Dow long-term options (LEAPS) on 10 of the 30 Dow stocks with highest dividends.

DEDICATION

I'd like to dedicate this newsletter to my lovely wife and daughter, and now grand-daughter who light up my life. It took a lot of time and effort to do all the research, writing, editing to write the books and now this newsletter.

The newsletter written for the Investor,
Written by the Investor, who cares about the Investor!

> *"Jeffrey Weber is great at explaining a sound investment strategy to help you save for a rainy day and build a legacy for the future."* Jacqi H.

THIS MONTH'S ANECDOTE
More Stock Market Reports

Golf carts are about par right now

Sand paper is having a rough time

Nails are taking a real hammering

Bolts are slipping but nuts are making a big turn around

Soap has been slipping badly, and shampoo is down a hair

Light bulb sales are dimming badly

Springs are bouncing back

Cracker sales are crumbling

The news on energy is just shocking

Dryers are spinning out of control

Washing machines are just going through their cycles.

"**Moral of the story**": Investors really need to take investing humorously!

AIM TIP OF THE MONTH – Stocks & LEAPS Recover from Bear Markets

Stock hit their all-time low in 1931 when the Dow Jones Industrial Index was at 31! One smart young investor who survived the Crash of 1929 was Bernard Baruch, one of the smartest investors who ever lived. When the Dow hit 31, he told his stockbroker to buy $10,000 worth of stock on all 30 stocks on the Dow Jones. His broker told him he was crazy – Baruch just said "do it!" Buying the 30 cost him $300,000 (probably $5 million in today's inflated dollars). That buy made him a multi-billionaire many years later.

He was one of the first people who unknowingly used the AIM contrary "Buy Low Sell High" strategy. It worked then and will work now! I've published this newsletter for 26 years. I dug up my old March 2009 newsletter and was amazed at the cheap prices. Then I looked up the prices on those same stocks in March 2018 – here is what I found:

Stock	Symbol	Mar 09 Price	Mar 09 Cost 100 Shares	Mar 19 Price	Mar 19 Cost 100 Shares
Caterpillar	CAT	$26.66	$2,666	$156.01	$15,601
Dow Chemical	DWDP	$8.10	$810	$69.07	$6,907
AT&T	T	$23.58	$2,358	$37.09	$3,709
China 25	FXI	$25.14	$2,514	$48.71	$4,871
Harley Davidson	HOG	$10.82	$1,082	$44.14	$4,414

BOOK REVIEW

The Money Spinner by Chuck Chakrapani (1990)

This is the description from Amazon with **my additional comments in bold.**

The book is divided into 8 Parts: (1) How *The Money Spinner* Can Make You Rich, (2) The Basic Principles Of *The Money Spinner*, (3) How To Set Up Your Own Money Spinner Program, (4) The Bottom Line: Does It Work? (5) For Investors With Special Requirements, (6) Some Questions Answered, (7) For The Absolute Beginner, and (8) A Final Word.

The Money Spinner by Chuck Chakrapani and Classic AIM (Automatic Investment Management) by Robert Lichello (in his book *How To Make $1,000,000 In The Stock Market Automatically*) are basically long-term investing systems that have a portfolio that is composed of cash and an investment instrument (i.e. stock, mutual funds, ETFs, gold, silver, convertible bonds, options, etc. **Jeff uses cash!**). If the investment instrument moves up beyond a trigger point, then some of the units of the investment instrument are sold and converted to cash; if the investment instrument moves down below a trigger point, then some of the cash is used to purchase units of the investment instrument. They are contrarian, buy-more-lower-and-sell-more-higher types of investing systems that depend on fluctuations and tell you when and how much to buy or sell.

The Money Spinner is more conservative than AIM when using standard settings. (Keep in mind that, in both systems, standard settings can be adjusted to user preferences. (**As Jeff has done with his Bear buying strategy!**) For example, when using my spreadsheets (which have a modification to prevent the running out of cash during downturns for both *The Money Spinner* and AIM) on Advanced Micro Devices Inc. (AMD) stock from month-end January 1991 to month-end January 2007, starting with $10,000: (1) Buy & Hold delivered ~$43,000 [annualized portfolio return = 9.5% per year], (2) AIM delivered ~$173,000 [annualized portfolio return = 19.4% per year], (3) The Money Spinner delivered ~$70,000 [annualized portfolio return = 12.8% per year] and (4) S&P 500 delivered ~$42,000 [annualized portfolio return = 9.4% per year].

The spreadsheets did not count interest, dividends, commissions and taxes. However, while the median amount of cash held by the AIM portfolio was ~47% - **Jeff says good amount!** Throughout the period, the median amount of cash held by *The Money Spinner* portfolio was ~63%, which is what I mean when I say that it is more conservative than AIM. (So *The Money Spinner*, when using standard settings, has a somewhat lower return but also a significantly dampened portfolio volatility which, when compared to AIM, allows one to sleep more soundly at night.) If one also looks at how *The Money Spinner* and AIM do the trading, then not counting the initial trade to set up both programs, one finds that for every $1 that *The Money Spinner* bought the AMD stock, it sold it for a weighted average price of 91% higher; whereas for AIM, for every $1 it bought the AMD stock, AIM sold it for a weighted average price of only 56% higher.

Three weaknesses of *The Money Spinner* and AIM are that: (1) both can run out of cash when using the systems by-the-book (**Jeff doesn't go by the book – I developed great Bear Strategy – you WON'T run out of cash!**), (2) both are dependent on when the strategy is started (i.e. since there is a large, initial component of the investment instrument, it is preferable to start the strategies when the value of the investment instrument is near a bottom (**exactly what I preach also)**, and (3) both depend on the investment instrument not losing all of its value.

The ideal investment instrument for both strategies is one that is easily marketable and has fluctuations as large as possible (**he couldn't know in 1990 but the stock market invented the perfect AIM investment – long-term options aka LEAPS)** and as frequent as possible. If the price of the investment instrument moves up linearly or exponentially over a long period of time, then Buy & Hold will beat both *The Money Spinner* and AIM. Neither system will generate profits if the price of the investment instrument remains in a thin trading range (**why I recommend LEAPS – not stocks).**

In addition, if one were to re-create these systems in a spreadsheet, I would say that *The Money Spinner* is relatively easier to create. (**Exactly why I create spreadsheets and send them to all my people I help with investing!)**

To sum up, if you want to eat well, use AIM, but if you want to sleep well, use *The Money Spinner*. You won't be buying low for this book – must be out-of-print – on Amazon cheapest price is $146.

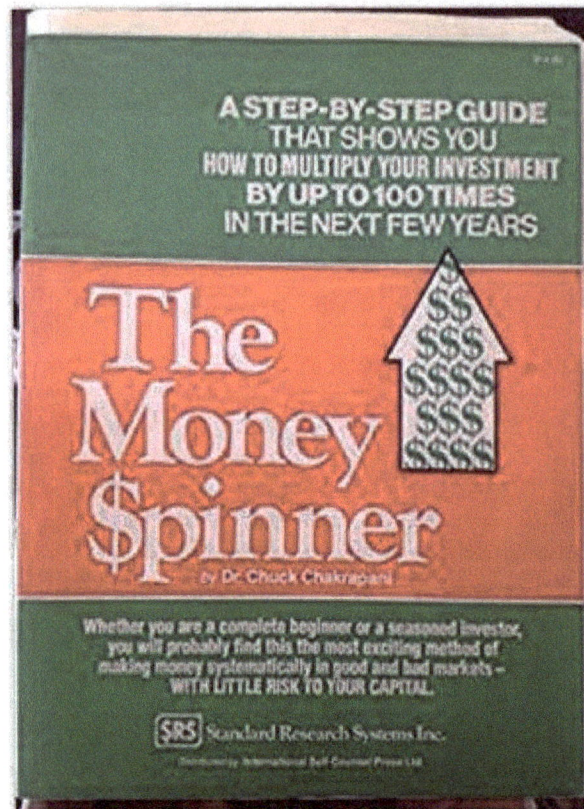

WEB SITE RECOMMENDATION

Zero Hedge - www.zerohedge.com

Here is a great site that my clients/friends can look at daily to find great articles related to investing and macro economics. Zero Hedge gives you a quick way to see financial daily headlines and commentaries that will make you a better AIM investor.

The JJJ INVESTING NEWSLETTER is published monthly by:

Jeff Weber of JJJ Investing Services, LLC
http://www.jjjinvesting.com

Ph # - 210 478-0655 (cell)
2302 Bluffridge St.
San Antonio, TX 78232

$150/YR for electronic version – contact me at **jeff@jjjinvesting.biz** to pay via PayPal.

The Philosophy for the Newsletter: give you safe, long-term investments (LEAPS)
that work well with AIM. I'll add a few words every month.

AIM REFERENCE WEB SITE

Below is a website with very useful information on the Dogs of the Dow stocks (Dogs are
the 10 Dow Jones stocks that pay highest dividends)

http://indexarb.com/dividendYieldSorteddj.html

DISCLAIMERS

I advise all readers to recognize that they can't assume all recommendations made in the future will be profitable or will equal the model portfolios shown in the newsletter. The information I give you is obtained from reliable sources but I can't guarantee the absolute accuracy of all the info. JJJ Investing Services is not a registered investment advisor and therefore cannot give individual investment advice. Some dates are Fiscal Year & some are Calendar Year. Remember when you see an "R" next to name of one of the good-buy stocks it means the stock is risky.

There are several important factors that go into deciding what stocks are good to use with AIM if you are looking for initial investments. Please read my book *Here Are the Customers' Yachts* (especially the BONUS section at the end) to learn what those are. (Remember, you shouldn't *ever* invest in anything before you understand WHAT you are doing and WHY.) Here are my Good Buy recommendations for this month. All of them have LEAPS.

AIM GOOD BUY RECOMMENDATIONS

These are selections I like and recommend looking at if you are starting with AIM now. To understand how I identify these picks, read my free book or my shorter, updated book on Amazon, *Here Are the Customers' Yachts*. All of these stocks have LEAPS:

Jet ADR - (JD)
IBM - (IBM)
Kraft Heinz - (KHC)
Starbucks - (SBUX)
Aurora Cannibis - (ACB)
Nio - (NIO)
eBay – (EBAY)
Facebook - (FB)
General Motors - (GM)
Macy's (M)
Micron Technology (MU
Advanced Micro Devices (AMD)

SPECIAL ANNOUNCEMENT: MY NEXT BOOK IS UNDERWAY

And I want to include as many newsletter subscribers as possible!

That means you!

[The rest of this section has been removed for the sake of this example.]

I have enjoyed writing this newsletter very much. Next are the model AIM portfolios I track and report every month. See you next month.

I am not a registered investing advisor and therefore cannot give you specific recommended stocks to buy. I can show you how the very safe Dow Jones Dogs of the Dow long-term LEAPS have done for the last 62 months and let you make up your own mind about whether they are the type of investment you want to choose to invest in.

When you are buying or selling long-term options (LEAPS) with your broker you will ALWAYS use these two transaction types - "Buy to Open" when buying options contracts and ALWAYS use "Sell to Close" when selling option contracts YOU WILL NEVER USE "SELL TO OPEN" OR "BUY TO CLOSE!!!!

And finally...

"To buy when others are despondently selling and to sell when others are avidly buying requires the greatest fortitude and pays the greatest ultimate rewards."

- **Sir John Templeton, 1958**

- JAN 21 DOW JONES Dogs of the Dow - LEAPS
JANUARY 2014 - MAY 2019

LEAPS NAME	OPTION PRICE	STARTING PORTFOLIO VALUE	CURRENT PORTFOLIO VALUE	% GAIN (LOSS)
JP MORGAN JAN 21 STRIKE 100 – JPM	14.62	6,000	56,517	842%
IBM JAN 21 STRIKE 140 – IBM	16.07	6,000	25,175	320%
PROCTOR & GAMBLE JAN 21 STRIKE 90 – PG	17.15	6,000	40,878	581%
CISCO JAN 21 STRIKE 40 – CSCO	16.55	6,000	64,048	968%
COCA-COLA JAN 21 STRIKE 40 – KO	7.68	6,000	19,459	224%
CHEVRON JAN 21 STRIKE 115 – CVX	17.85	6,000	34,981	483%
EXXON MOBIL JAN 21 STRIKE 75 – XOM	10.75	6,000	19,909	232%
MERCK JAN 21 STRIKE 70 – MRK	14.75	6,000	39,089	552%
PFIZER JAN 21 STRIKE 40 – PFE	5.70	6,000	23,082	285%
VERIZON JAN 21 STRIKE 55 – VZ	7.12	6,000	27,896	367%
TOTALS		**$60,000**	**$351,034**	**485%**

Our Dogs of the Dow Jones LEAPS are now up to 485%, **UP 65%** this month in a very bullish month! Many good buys! We switched to 2021 LEAPS rolling over the 2020 LEAPS – did this with all model portfolios. Dogs dropped Boeing & Caterpillar & added JP Morgan & Proctor & Gamble.

This is investing for the long haul - not day trading. We switched to 2021 LEAPS for all LEAPS in January 2019 on all model LEAPS portfolios.

I am not a registered investing advisor and therefore cannot give you specific recommended stocks to buy. I can show you how the very safe Dow Jones Dogs of the Dow long-term options (LEAPS) have done for the last 62 months and let you make up your own mind about whether they are the type of investment you want to choose to invest in.

DOW JONES STOCKS
SEPTEMBER 1993 - MAY 2019

STOCK NAME	STOCK	PORTFOLIO	% GAIN
	PRICE	TOTAL	(LOSS)
ALTRIA	54.77	25,396	1593%
AM EXPRESS	110.96	27,859	1757%
COCA-COLA	46.46	9,887	559%
DISNEY	115.00	22,971	1431%
GENERAL ELECTRIC	10.01	2,898	93%
CITIBANK	65.55	6,263	109%
IBM	143.28	25,022	1568%
MONDELEZ	49.68	5,240	136%
MCDONALDS	190.71	25,311	1587%
MERCK	81.45	12,391	726%
PHILIP MORRIS	85.44	IN ALTRIA	IN ALTRIA
TOTALS		$163,238	988%

We will keep our original Dow Jones Portfolio which includes both dogs and non-Dogs of the Dow. Portfolio up 23% this month to 988% in BULLISH month for these stocks and up 988% since beginning in 1993!

I have started including dividends!

DOW JONES DOGS OF THE DOW - STOCKS
JANUARY 2014 - MAY 2019

NAME	STOCK	PORTFOLIO	% GAIN
	PRICE	TOTAL	(LOSS)
COCA-COLA	46.47	10,108	69%
CHEVRON	126.42	10,279	71%
PROCTOR & GAMBLE	103.65	12,159	103%
CISCO	55.21	10,997	83%
IBM	143.28	10,205	70%
JP MORGAN	140.36	11,057	84%
EXXON MOBIL	82.49	8,515	42%
MERCK	81.15	10,494	75%
PFIZER	42.99	9,398	57%
VERIZON	59.09	8,441	41%
TOTALS		$101,653	70%

This portfolio is the new 2019 DOG OF THE DOW STOCKS portfolio. I think this portfolio will work well over the long haul. Portfolio is up 4% this month to 70% from last month. This was a bullish month.

JAN 21 IN THE MONEY LEAPS
AUGUST 2006 - MAY 2019

LEAPS NAME	OPTION PRICE	STARTING PORTFOLIO VALUE	CURRENT PORTFOLIO VALUE	% GAIN (LOSS)
AMAZON JAN 21 STRIKE 1600 – AMZN	459.08	132,750	3,826,486	2783%
AM EXPRESS JAN 21 STRIKE 100 – AXP	20.70	205,000	147,190	(28%)
CATERPILLAR JAN 21 STRIKE 110 – CAT	37.50	236,250	386,095	64%
COCA-COLA JAN 21 STRIKE 40 – KO	7.68	73,500	632,937	761%
DISNEY JAN 21 STRIKE 100 – DIS	24.48	60,000	563,764	840%
GENERAL ELEC JAN 21 STRIKE 3 – GE	7.00	77,375	10,906	(86%)
IBM JAN 21 STRIKE 110 – IBM	35.25	141,000	188,934	34%
MONDELEZ JAN 21 STRIKE 35 – MDLZ	15.70	36,750	519,749	1314%
APPLE JAN 21 STRIKE 125 – AAPL	66.90	72,750	2,501,373	3338%
MERCK JAN 21 STRIKE 65 – MRK	18.62	81,000	330,327	308%
TOTALS		**$1,116,375**	**$9,216,446**	**726%**

We switched from Jan 2020 to Jan 2021 LEAPS. Jan 21 In The Money Call LEAPS UP AN INCREDIBLE 122%! to 726% this month due to sharp RISE in MANY LEAPS We have plenty of cash, LEAPS UP a total of 726%, since August 2006. We count six months owned Jan 08 LEAPS which includes profit of $138,685 carried over from previous Jan 08 in the money LEAPS. I switched from Altria to Amazon as I feel Amazon is the better company for the future & switched McDonalds for Apple in April.

In the money merely means that the stock is currently at a higher price than the Strike price listed. Will add the $138,685 profit made from the 08s we held for 6 months to figure gains. We added Kraft because Altria spun off Kraft giving Altria shareholders .7 shares of Kraft for each share of Altria owned. Again readjusted several LEAPS and added to number of contracts owned.

Motley Fool - Dogs of the Dow 2014

Wikipedia article on Dogs of the Dow

Buffalo News article on Dogs of the Dow

CNBC Dogs of the Dow 2013

Forbes Dogs of the Dow

FAANGS is the acronym for Facebook, Apple, Amazon, Netflix, and Google (now Alphabet)

JAN 21 Portfolio Has Chinese, Some Big Names, JANUARY 2016 - MAY 2019

LEAPS NAME	OPTION	STARTING	CURRENT	% GAIN
	PRICE	PORTFOLIO VALUE	PORTFOLIO VALUE	(LOSS)
CHINA 25 JAN 21 STRIKE 30 – FXI	16.28	100,000	214,382	114%
NIKE JAN 21 STRIKE 50 – NKE	37.65	100,000	209,672	110%
AMAZON JAN 21 STRIKE 1800 – AMZN	346.60	100,000	677,968	578%
ALPHABET JAN 21 STRIKE 1300 – GOOG	135.90	100,000	251,210	151%
AMD JAN 21 STRIKE 20 – AMD	13.20	100,000	61,850	(38%)
TESLA (PUT) JAN 21 STRIKE 210 – TSLA	42.08	100,000	80,036	(20%)
FACEBOOK JAN 21 STRIKE 150 – FB	45.92	100,000	165,849	66%
PAYPAL JAN 21 STRIKE 75 – PYPL	37.58	100,000	571,193	471%
APPLE JAN 21 STRIKE 150 – AAPL	55.23	100,000	521,737	422%
ALIBABA JAN 21 STRIKE 150 – BABA	54.20	100,000	387,622	288%
TOTALS		**$1,000,000**	**$3,141,519**	**214%**

Here's a new portfolio that has several of the big boys of the stock market and includes one put on stock I think will go down before going up. UP 44% to 214% this month in BULLISH market for FAANGS, again some good buys. Again changed all LEAPS to 2021 LEAPS and readjusted cash/LEAPS ratio back to 50% - 50% & adjusted Strike prices up or down depending on what the stock did in 2018.

JAN 21 Portfolio Has Out of Money Dow Jones Industrial Average LEAPS
SEPTEMBER 2016 – MAY 2019

LEAPS NAME	OPTION	STARTING	CURRENT	% GAIN
	PRICE	PORTFOLIO VALUE	PORTFOLIO VALUE	(LOSS)
VERIZON JAN 21 STRIKE 60 – VZ	4.60	10,000	37,544	275%
CATERPILLAR JAN 21 STRIKE 130 – CAT	25.00	10,000	49,813	399%
PFIZER JAN 21 STRIKE 40 – PFE	5.70	10,000	17,875	79%
GENERAL ELECTRIC JAN 21 STRIKE 8	3.32	19,000	6,558	(34%)
INTEL JAN 21 STRIKE 50 – INTC	10.65	10,000	46,955	370%
MICROSOFT JAN 21 STRIKE 110 – MSFT	21.02	10,000	45,696	357%
DOW DUPONT JAN 21 STRIKE 65 – DPDW	3.48	10,000	9,993	0%
NIKE JAN 21 STRIKE 85 – NKE	12.45	10,000	20,131	101%
MERCK JAN 21 STRIKE 85 – MRK	6.25	10,000	12,898	29%
COCA-COLA JAN 21 STRIKE 45 – KO	4.38	10,000	12,264	23%
TOTALS		$109,000	$259,677	138%

This is a new portfolio. To help smaller investors I have started a portfolio with cheaper priced Dow Jones LEAPS by picking lower cost shares and buying LEAPS slightly Out of the Money (the Strike prices are higher than the stock price) Let's see how they do! Up 27% this month, UP to 138% total in BULLISH month.

I am not a registered investing advisor and therefore cannot give specific recommendations on individual stocks to buy. I can help you make sure you are doing the method correctly and give you ideas on how to make the highest profits possible. If you are interested in my management/education services please contact me at jeff@jjjinvesting.biz.

JAN 21 Wealthy Portfolio Has FAANG, FAANG-LIKE-LEAPS
April 2019 – MAY 2019

LEAPS NAME	OPTION	STARTING	CURRENT	% GAIN
	PRICE	PORTFOLIO VALUE	PORTFOLIO VALUE	(LOSS)
GOLDMAN SACHS JAN 21 STRIKE 205 – GS	28.25	1,648,800	1,676,062	2%
AMAZON JAN 21 STRIKE 1750 – AMZN	372.48	3,280,000	3,510,600	7%
ALIBABA JAN 21 STRIKE 180 – BABA	37.00	2,080,800	2,155,600	4%
APPLE JAN 21 STRIKE 165 – AAPL	46.35	1,583,200	1,722,558	9%
TESLA JAN 21 (PUT) STRIKE 300 – TSLA	84.82	3,742,000	3,576755	(4%)
MICROSOFT JAN 21 STRIKE 100 – MSFT	27.88	1,072,000	1,096,280	2%
PAYPAL JAN 21 STRIKE 90 – PYPL	26.90	506,000	523,265	4%
ALPHABET JAN 21 STRIKE 1175 – GOOG	195.26	3,870,000	3,897,335	1%
BERKSHIRE HATHAWAY JAN 21 STRIKE 200 – BRK.B	30.88	1,726,800	1,794,117	4%
AMGEN JAN 21 STRIKE 190 – AMGN	25.20	958,400	985,596	3
TOTALS		$20,468,000	20,938,168	2.3%

This is my new FAANG, FAANG-LIKE LEAPS Portfolio for wealthier investors. AIM loves wealthy investors too and will take good care of you. In 3 weeks up 2.3% which equals a 39% annual rate of return. Follow along and see how this portfolio grows.

I wrote this newsletter myself, and it expresses my own opinions. I am not receiving compensation for it other than from subscribers. I have no business relationship with any company whose stock is mentioned in this article.

Additional disclosure: The author of this article is not an investment adviser and gives only his personal view and opinion, never making any investment advice or recommendation to buy or sell specific securities. Investors in financial assets must do so at their own responsibility and with due caution as they involve a significant degree of risk. Before investing in financial assets, investors should do their own research and consult a professional investment adviser.

Additional disclosure: Investors are always reminded that before making any investment, you should do your own proper due diligence on any name directly or indirectly mentioned in this article. Investors should also consider seeking advice from a broker or financial adviser before making any investment decisions. Any material in this article should be considered general information, and not relied on as a formal investment recommendation.

And finally...

"To buy when others are despondently selling and to sell when others are avidly buying requires the greatest fortitude and pays the greatest ultimate rewards."

-Sir John Templeton, 1958

I hope you enjoyed reading this example of a monthly newsletter. I have put a lot of work into it each and every month for the past 26 years.

You may have seen that I used to only charge $15 / year for the newsletter. In 2018 the rate is $150 / year considering the unique value that it provides. Even $1,500 / year makes sense when you consider that you are being given many portfolios and a method that produces such unbeatable results, safely and legally.

Your eyes should have gotten wide when you saw that the Dogs of the Dow LEAPS portfolio has increased 420% in just over 5 years!

What can you achieve in the next 5 years using AIM with LEAPS? Ask me for a complimentary trial period subscription this newsletter by sending me an email at jeff@jjjinvesting.biz or going to the FREE OFFERS page on my website: www.jjjinvesting.com.

Working with Jeff began as one small step for this man, which then grew into tremendous LEAPS forward for my life - and for the investing community. Thanks for all that you do, Jeff!

Brett Hoffstadt, Jeff's business partner and former aerospace project manager

APPENDIX

What Clients Get from JJJ Investing Services

How Jeff Helps You Manage Your New AIM Portfolio

I offer you six months of AIM management services for an incredibly reasonable fee based on your portfolio value. You are probably wondering what you get for my management fee. I will tell you!

First I will phone you or visit with you in person (if you are in San Antonio, Texas) to explain basic AIM strategy to you so you understand how AIM works.

Then I will ask you how much money you want to start off with and give you recommendations on current stocks I like and the Strike prices of long-term options (LEAPS) on those stocks I like.

Then I will help you open an account with a stock broker and coach you on how to answer the questions you are asked. I recommend TD Ameritrade because I use them and if you also use TD Ameritrade I can easily walk you through and buys or sells on your LEAPS.

After you open your account you will send money to the broker to fund your account.

It usually takes about three more days before the funds you sent the broker are allowed to be used to trade options. Options are non-marginal so the broker waits until your funds are cleared and then you can trade options.

Once you can buy options I will walk you through your first purchases. All beginning and future buys and sells will be at limit prices. So for example the LEAPS I want you to buy closed at $34.00 an option or $3,400 a contract. I might tell you put in a limit buy order at $32.50 for the LEAPS or $32,500 to buy 10 contracts.

I create a spreadsheet for you with this limit buy price. This spreadsheet shows your opening buy information. At the bottom of the spreadsheet will be your next buy and sell prices – if you first bought at $3,250 a contract, your next buy will be around $2,250 and your first sell will be at around $4,500.

Once I create the spreadsheet I look up the closing price of your LEAPS every day the stock market is open. Then every evening I can phone you to tell you how your LEAPS did that day, whether you have a buy, a sell or do nothing. Once your LEAPS start getting close to a buy or sell, I strongly urge you to put in a limit order to buy or sell.

Whenever you have a buy or sell I update your spreadsheet with the buy or sell, figure new buy and sell prices and email you the new spreadsheet.

Brokers let you keep limit order open for three months when you say Good till Cancelled.

Every day when I call I explain little bits about AIM and continue your education about why I recommend doing this or that. I want you to get smarter about AIM and eventually I want you to feel comfortable about doing AIM solo…and I will get you there!

You are always welcome to email or phone me with any questions about AIM you have.

I even have a Bear strategy when particular stocks (like GE & IBM lately) start going bearish that helps save your cash and buy at the lowest possible prices.

At the end of every month I update your spreadsheet with the end of the month price on your LEAPS so you see how you are doing.

This description cannot do justice to all I do for my clients/friends. You need to hire me and see for yourself. You will find me funny, knowledgeable, and very friendly. I love helping people.

AIM Management Fees

My fees are based on how much I help you grow your portfolio over six months with AIM. I provide this help for six months at a time so that you can hopefully learn how to do it yourself after that. But some people enjoy my help and conversation so much that they are long-term clients.

Please go to my website www.jjjinvesting.com to see my current rates since this book may be purchased long after 2019.

Newsletter

Newsletter will be free for a limited period if you contact me. It is currently $150 a year for renewals (in 2019).

My Other Books on AIM

I Guarantee You will Buy Low Sell High and Make Money (Available as a FREE PDF)

Here Are the Customers Yachts - $4.95 eBook & $15.95 Paperback. Buy it on Amazon.

Jeff, your service is well worth the money (hell of a lot more as a matter of fact). Thank you for your special treatment of me.
Walt M. - U.S. Air Force Colonel (retired)

ABOUT THE AUTHOR

Jeffrey Weber was born in the Bronx, a borough of New York City. His publishing experience started at age 18 when his first article was published in Railroad Model Craftsman magazine. The year was 1965. Jeff soon went to college at the University of Arizona and received a Bachelor's Degree in History & Government. After continuing into law school for a year and a half, he transferred to the University of Nevada, Las Vegas, and obtained a Bachelor's degree in Accounting.

While at the University of Arizona, Jeff hunted inside used bookstores for books on investing. One day he found the perfect book: *How to Make $1,000,000 in the Stock Market Automatically* by Robert Lichello. Jeff liked his book so much that he started getting ideas on how he could write his own book and improve on the ideas that Mr. Lichello invented.

After college, Jeff was drafted into the U.S. Army. For 33 years he worked for the US Army and the US Air Force as an auditor and management analyst. He is a proud draftee who fought in the Vietnam War.

Jeff's first book on investing was written under strange conditions about as far away as you can get from the New York stocks markets – in Tunduchan, Korea; (10 miles from demilitarized zone or DMZ), in Maffle, Belgium; and in Weilerbach, Germany. For 17 years, Jeff was stationed overseas. It was in these cities that Jeff also began developing and delivering workshops to his fellow soldiers and their families about the AIM method from Lichello.

Jeff's audiences appreciated one benefit of Lichello's strategy - it doesn't require you to be near the stock market to use it. In the years since his deployments, Jeff has improved on the simplicity and effectiveness of the original AIM method by adding a Bear Strategy and by expanding the method into long-term stock options (LEAPS).

Since 1993, Jeff has produced and provided a monthly newsletter on investing. His first investing book (available now for free) was written over twenty years ago. His second book, *Here Are the Customers' Yachts*, was published in 2017.

Jeff is currently semi-retired, dedicating all of his available time and resources to help as many people as possible benefit from AIM as a safe, reliable, and profitable way to invest. In the 2014 timeframe, JJJ Investing Services brought on a business and publication partner to improve the website, newsletter, and book publication services.

Jeff is the world's leading investor and teacher of AIM with long-term options (LEAPS). How can we say this? At least 10 times Jeff has been the only buyer or seller of LEAPS contracts for a particular company and Strike Price. When you see JD LEAPS Jan 2021 Strike 30 sold 5 contracts - those were his 5 contracts! His teaching is done through several outlets: workshops, 1-on-1 training, videos, video chat, website blog, and books such as the one you are reading now.

Since Jeff is the only person teaching how to use AIM with long-term options, he feels a special obligation to share his knowledge. This third book adds and improves on his latest wisdom, provides special insights for wealthy investors, and contains improved instructions for any investor to become proficient - and profitable - with the AIM method. With *AIM for Millions with Stock Options*, you are given what you need to become the best AIM investor you can be.